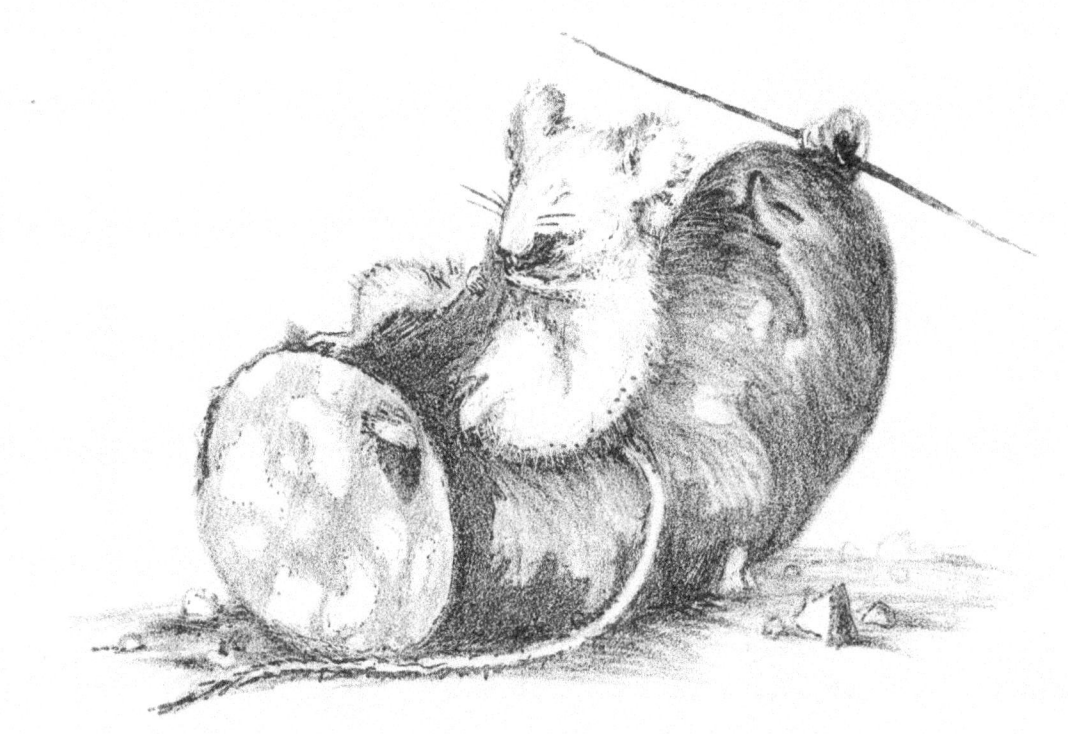

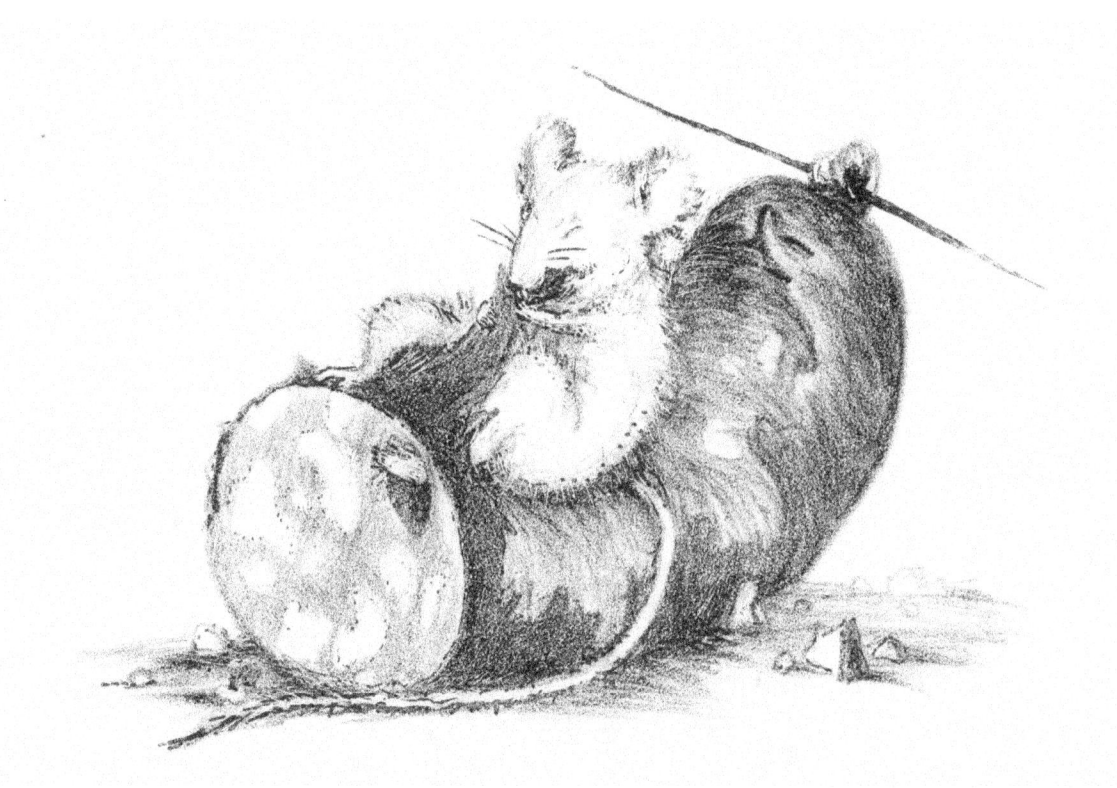

Elena Abdulaeva

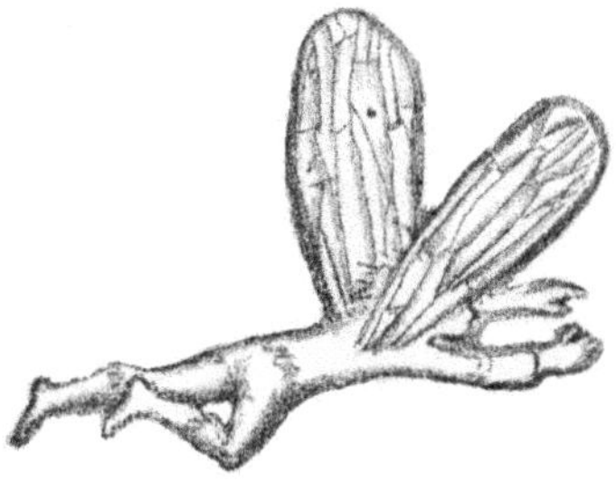

Andersen's Unknown Fairy Tales

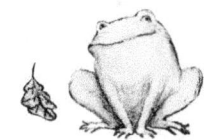

Grayscale Coloring Book

Elena Abdulaeva
Andersen's Unknown Fairy Tales
Grayscale Coloring Book

Series of Illustrations by Elena Abdulaeva
Stone Lithography, 2006-2007
Scanned from Paper Originals, 2016

Published by Elena Abdulaeva, www.abdulaeva.com.
Printed by CreateSpace, an Amazon.com company.
Available at Amazon.com and other retailers.

Fine Art Prints available from art.abdulaeva.com

ISBN-13: 978-1543083576
ISBN-10: 1543083579

Classic Fairy Tales

in Stone Lithography

The lithographic process was born in the 18th century. Since then, through constant modification and improvement, it has remained with us and it is the most important large-scale printing technology today.

However, in its original, craft version, it was not just a new reproduction method; the texture of the stone itself became part of the artwork, lending to the picture its rough magic and allowing the artist to create images with unique and subtle character.

Stone lithography today is as long and laborious a process as it was 200 years ago; but it is the ultimate colorist's dream. The black-and-white original litho print provides the freedom for the artist to experiment with the coloring, while the stone grain and irregularities provide the beautiful underlying texture, impossible to achieve by any other means.

Now you can enjoy coloring the same art pieces that went into the printed edition of the "Unknown Fairy Tales" that I illustrated. Feel free to reproduce my version or to realize your own vision—each image is printed twice. I hope you will enjoy coloring these pictures as much as I enjoyed creating and coloring them myself. Good luck!

Elena Abdulaeva

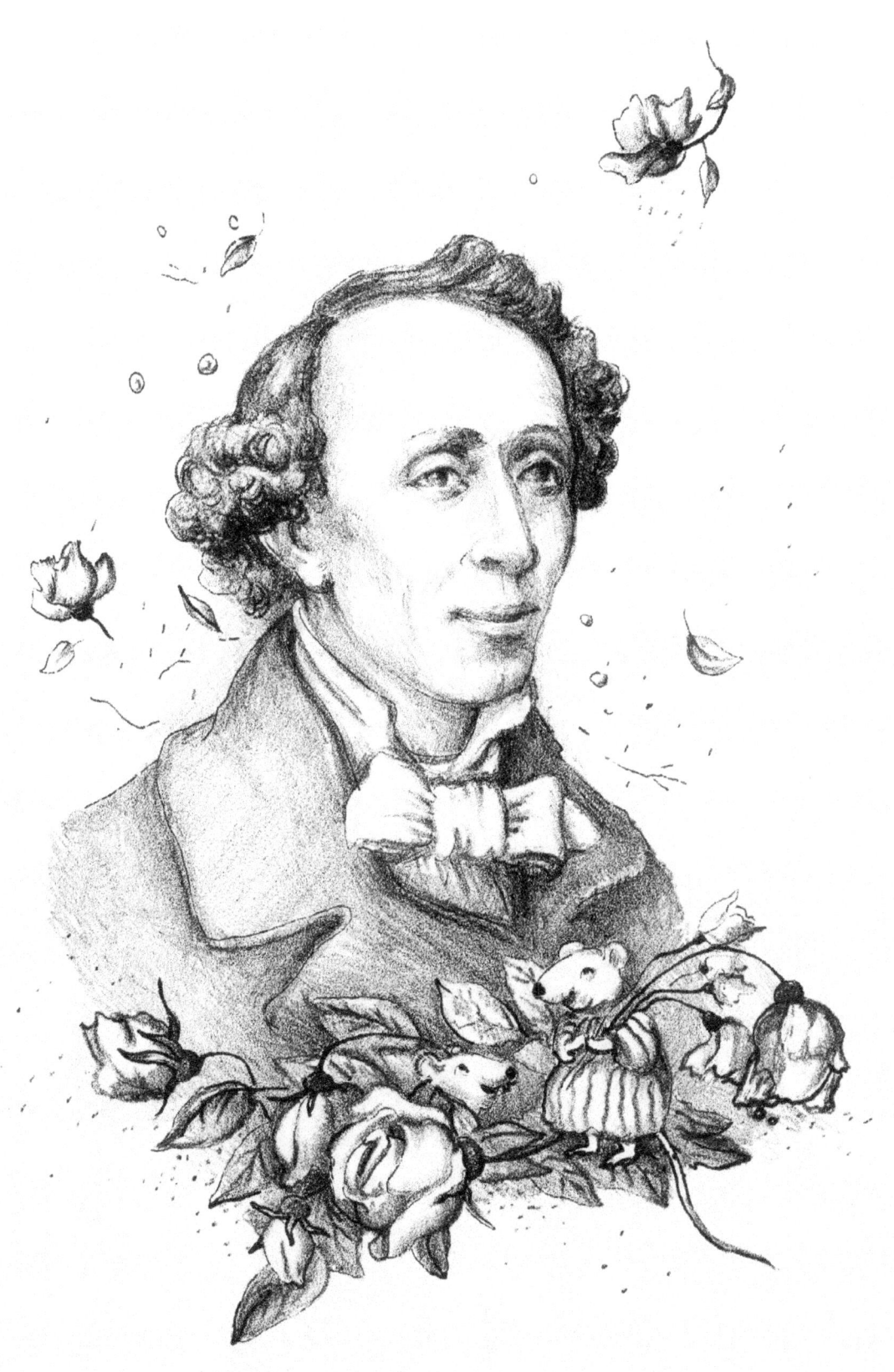

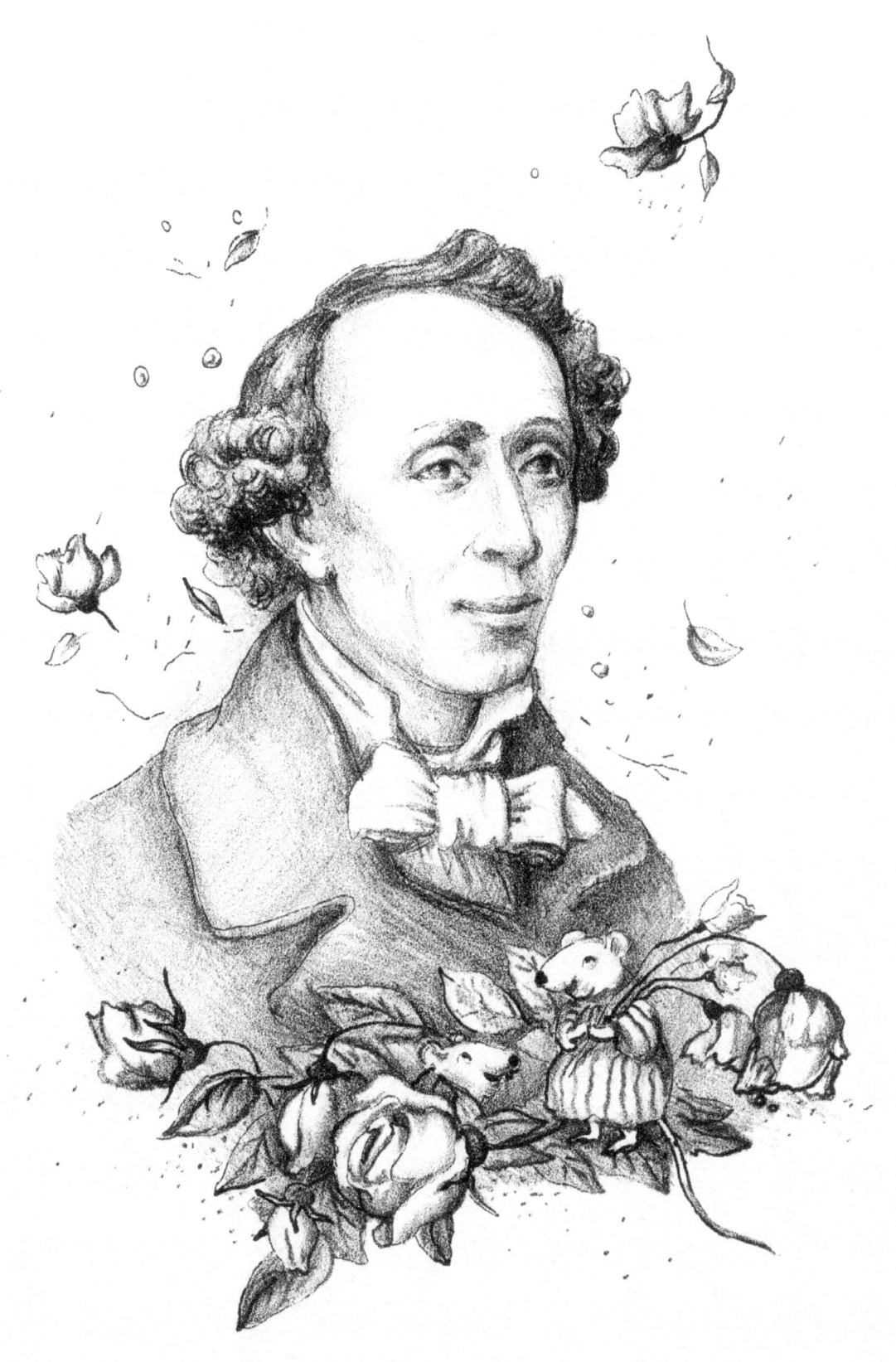

Soup from a Sausage Peg

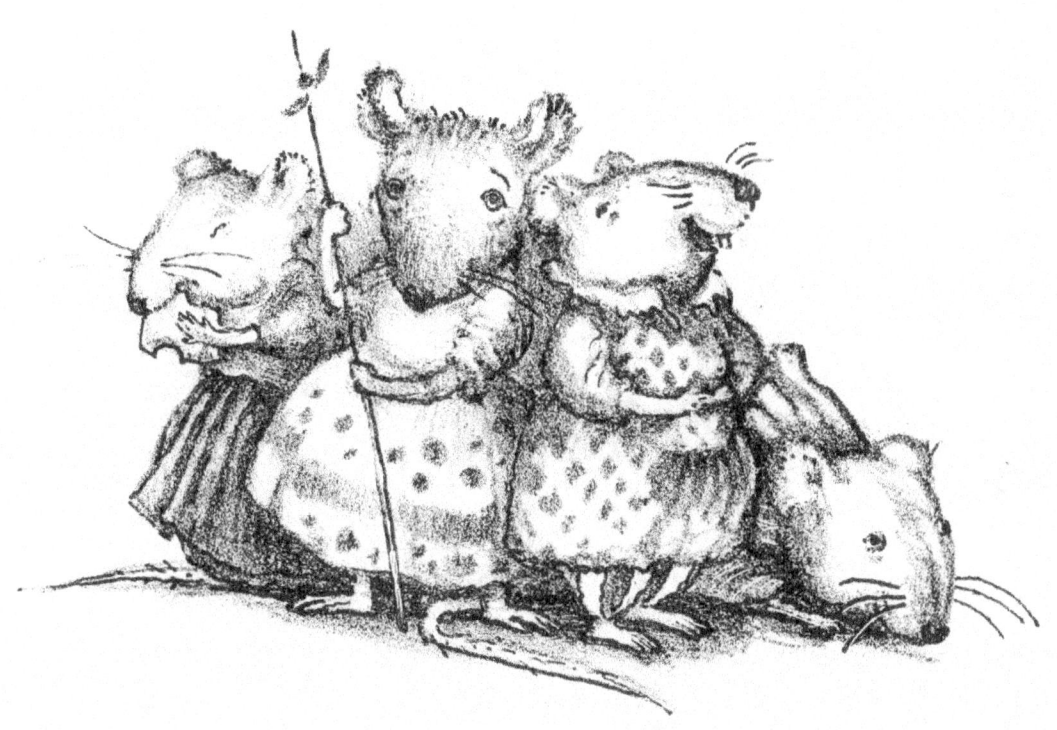

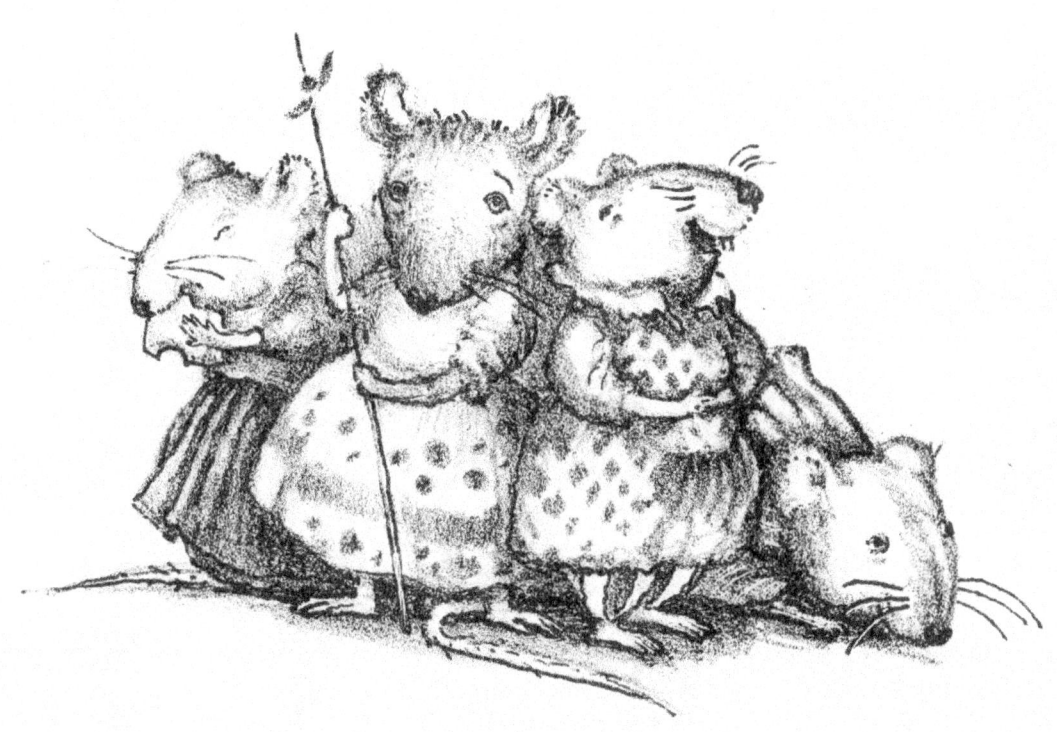

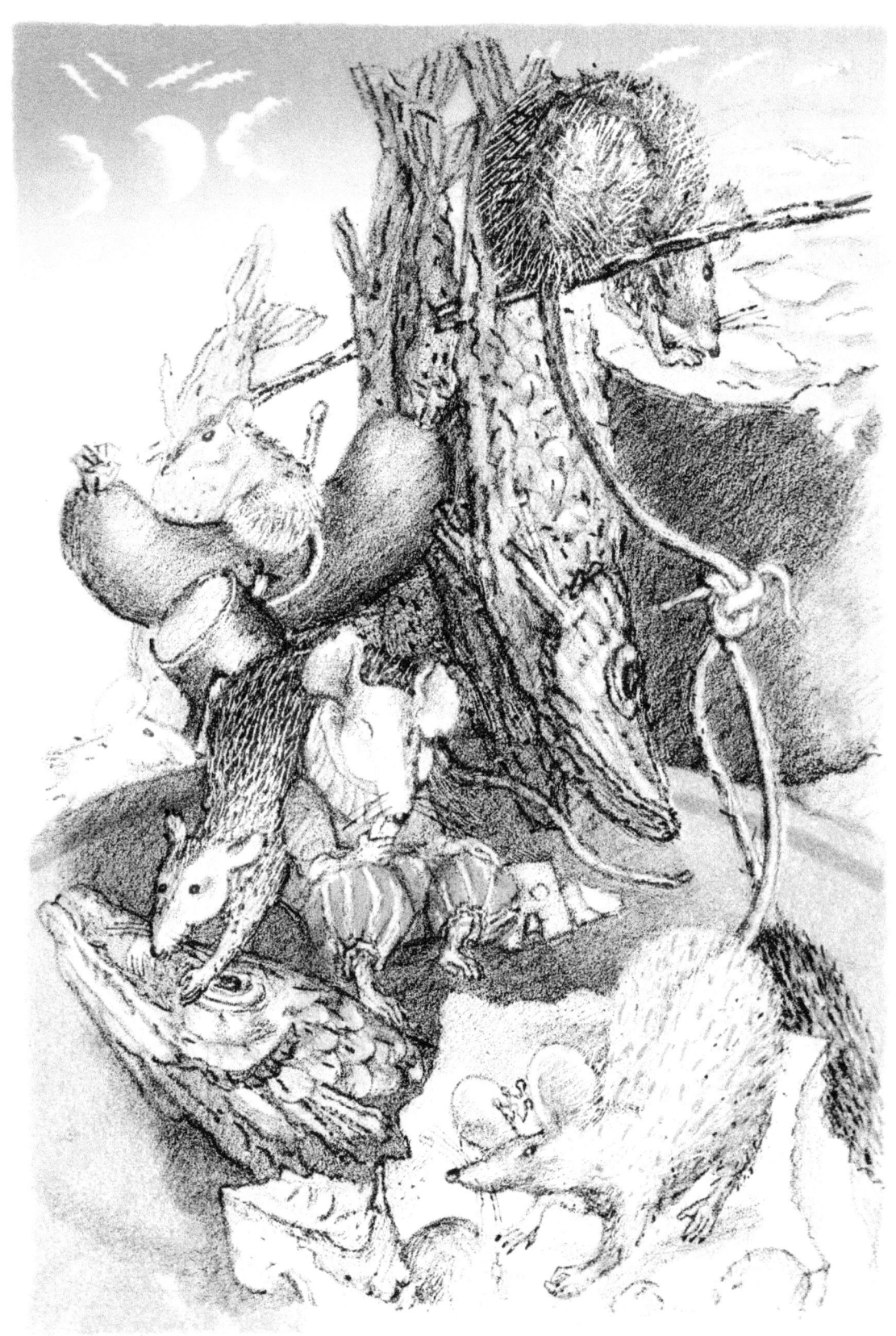

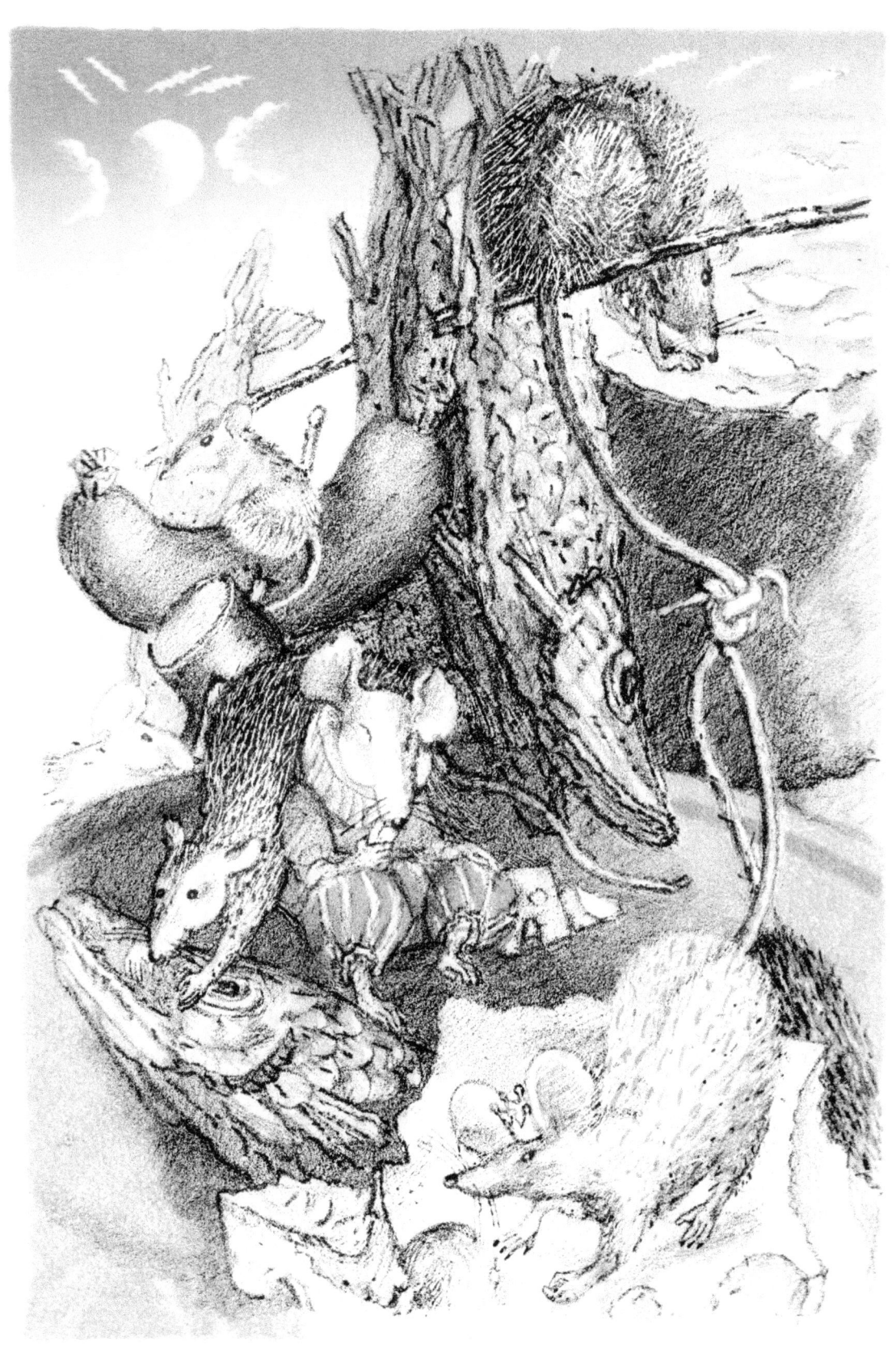

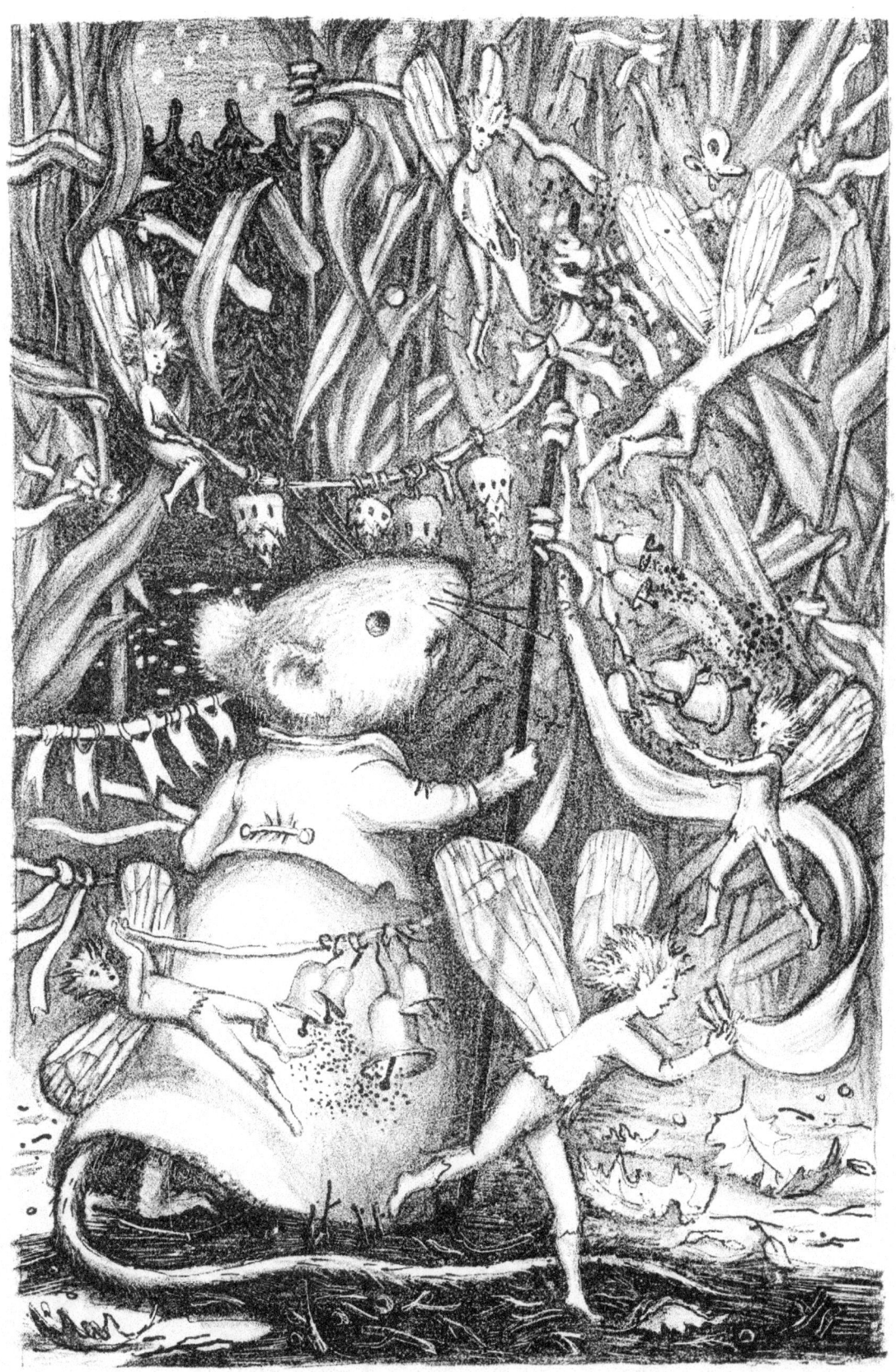

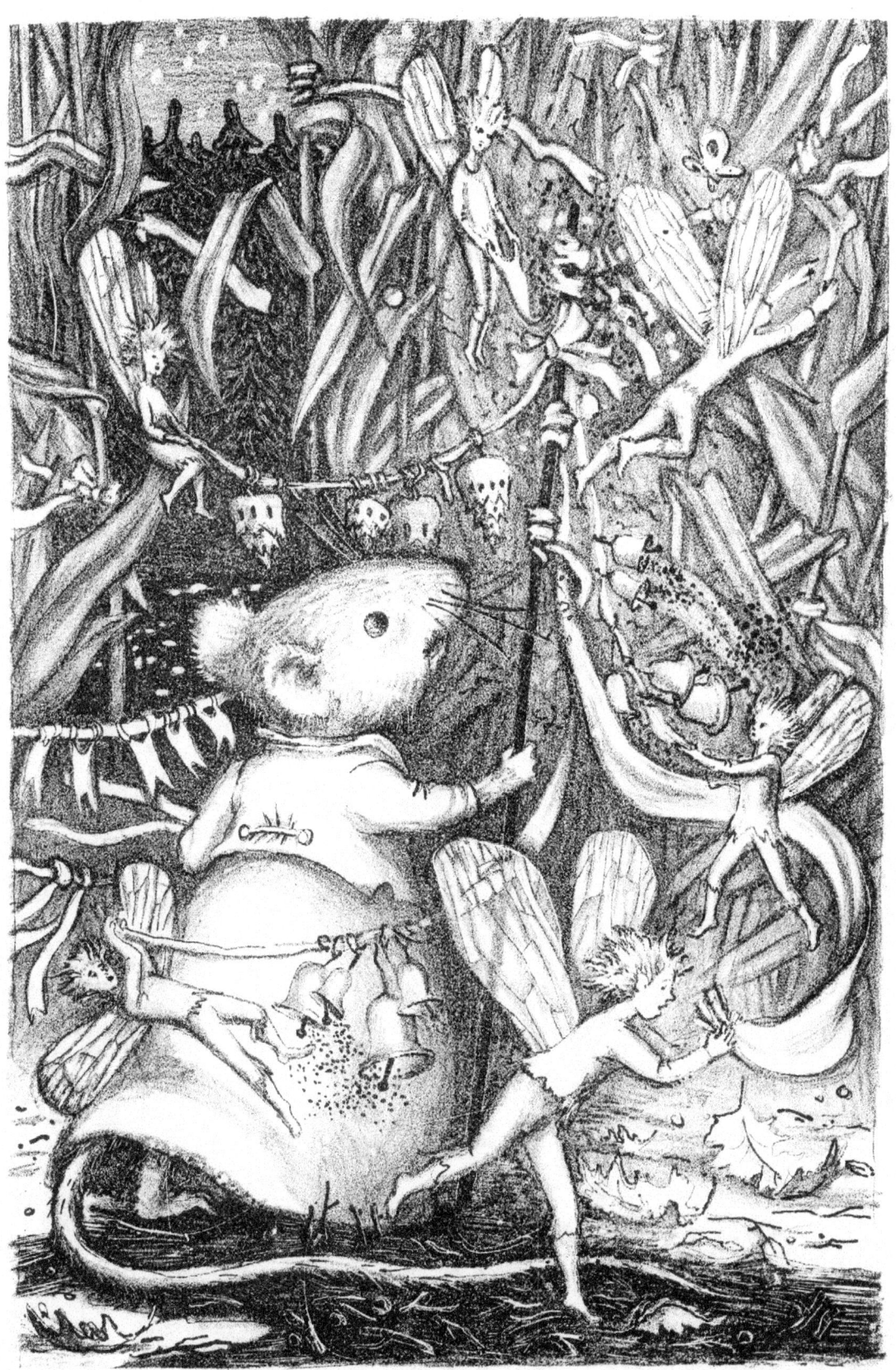

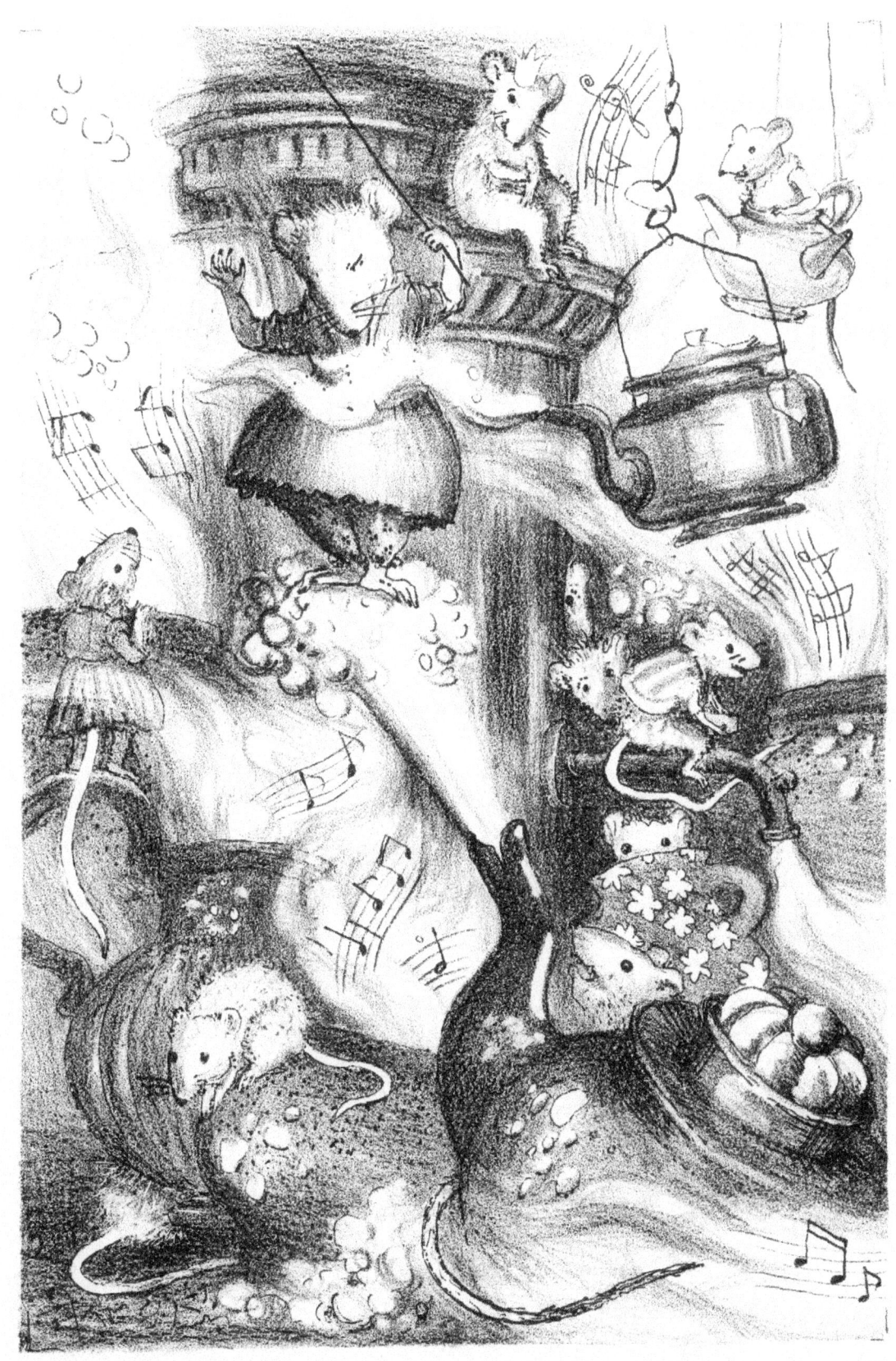

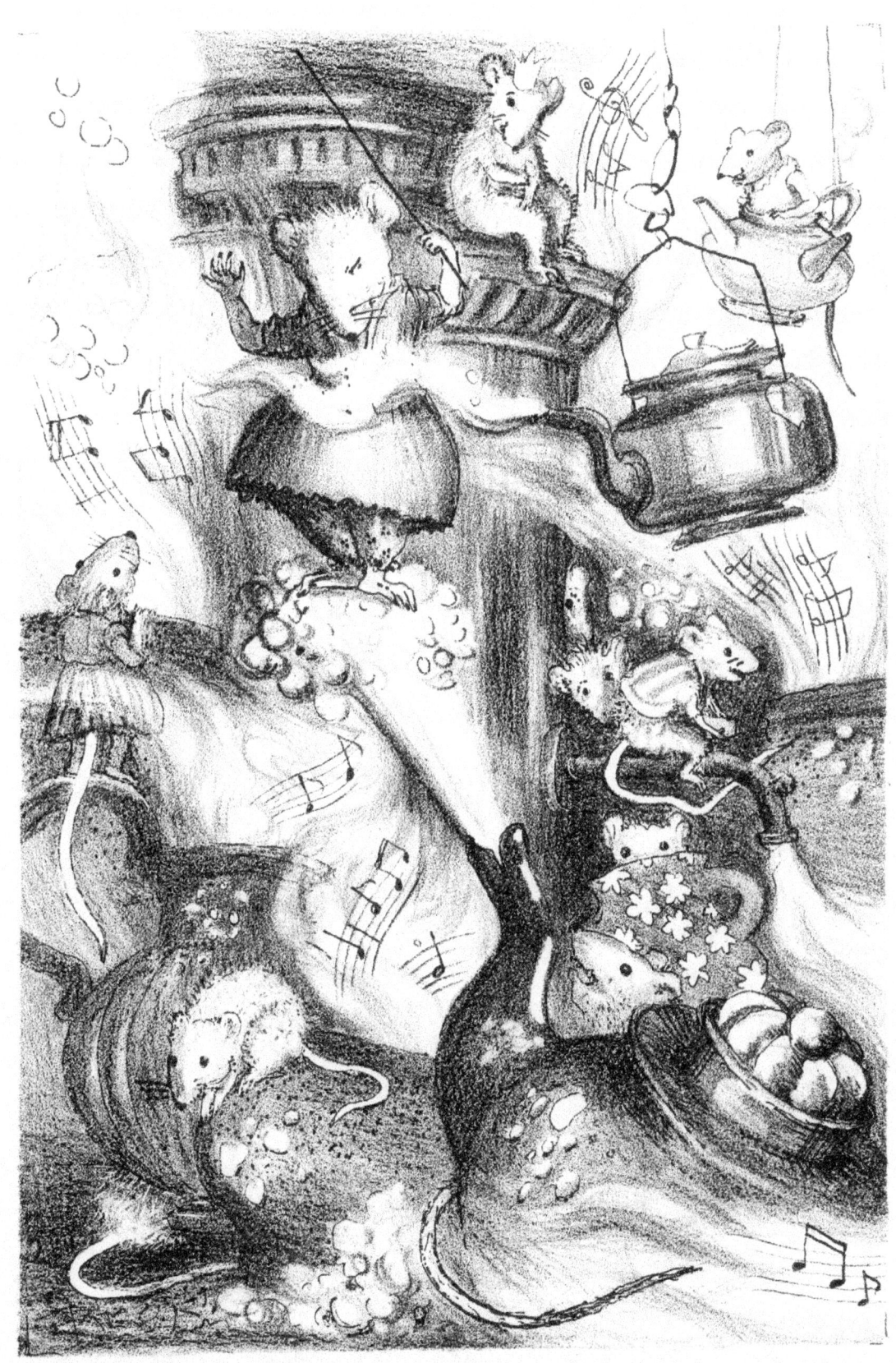

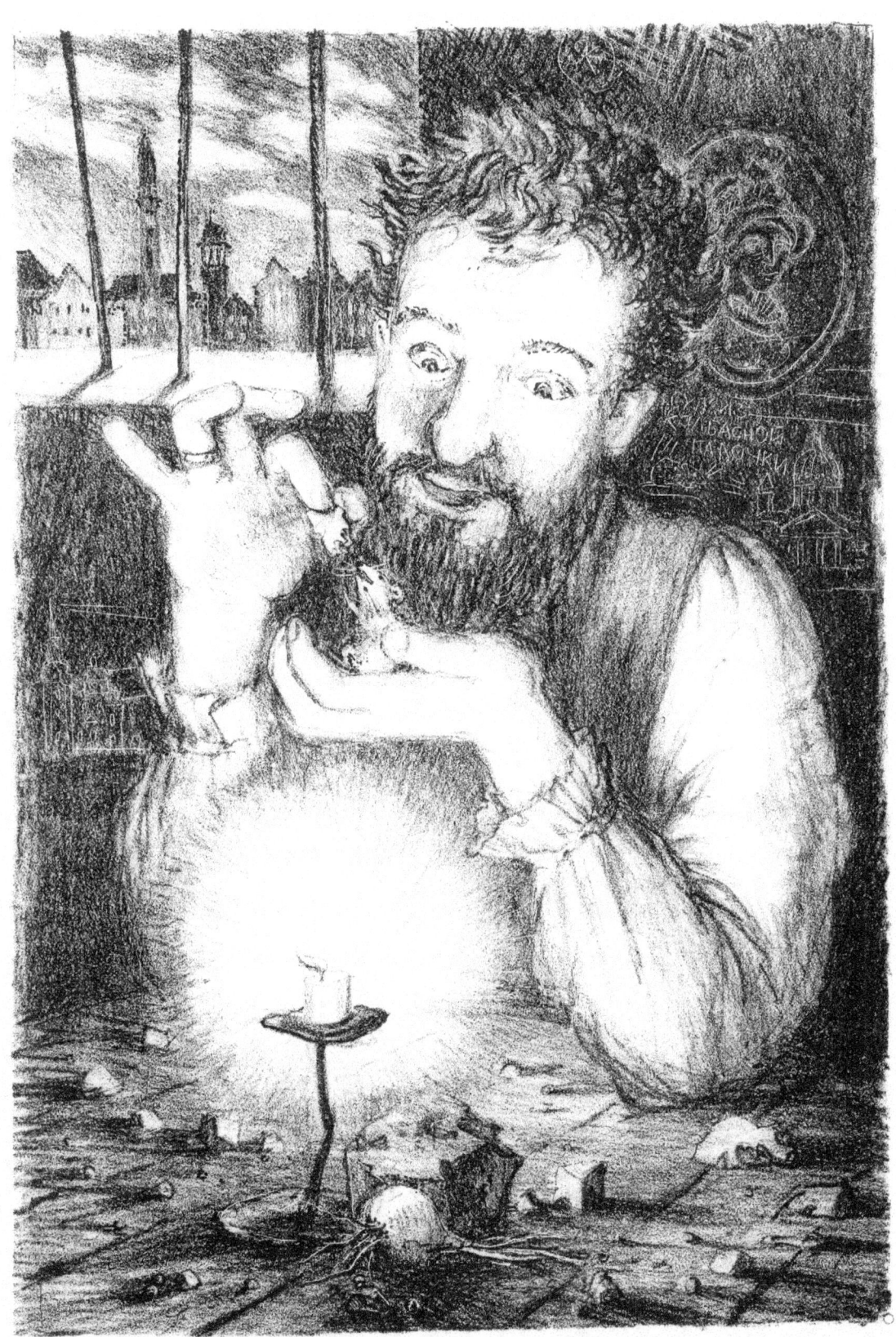

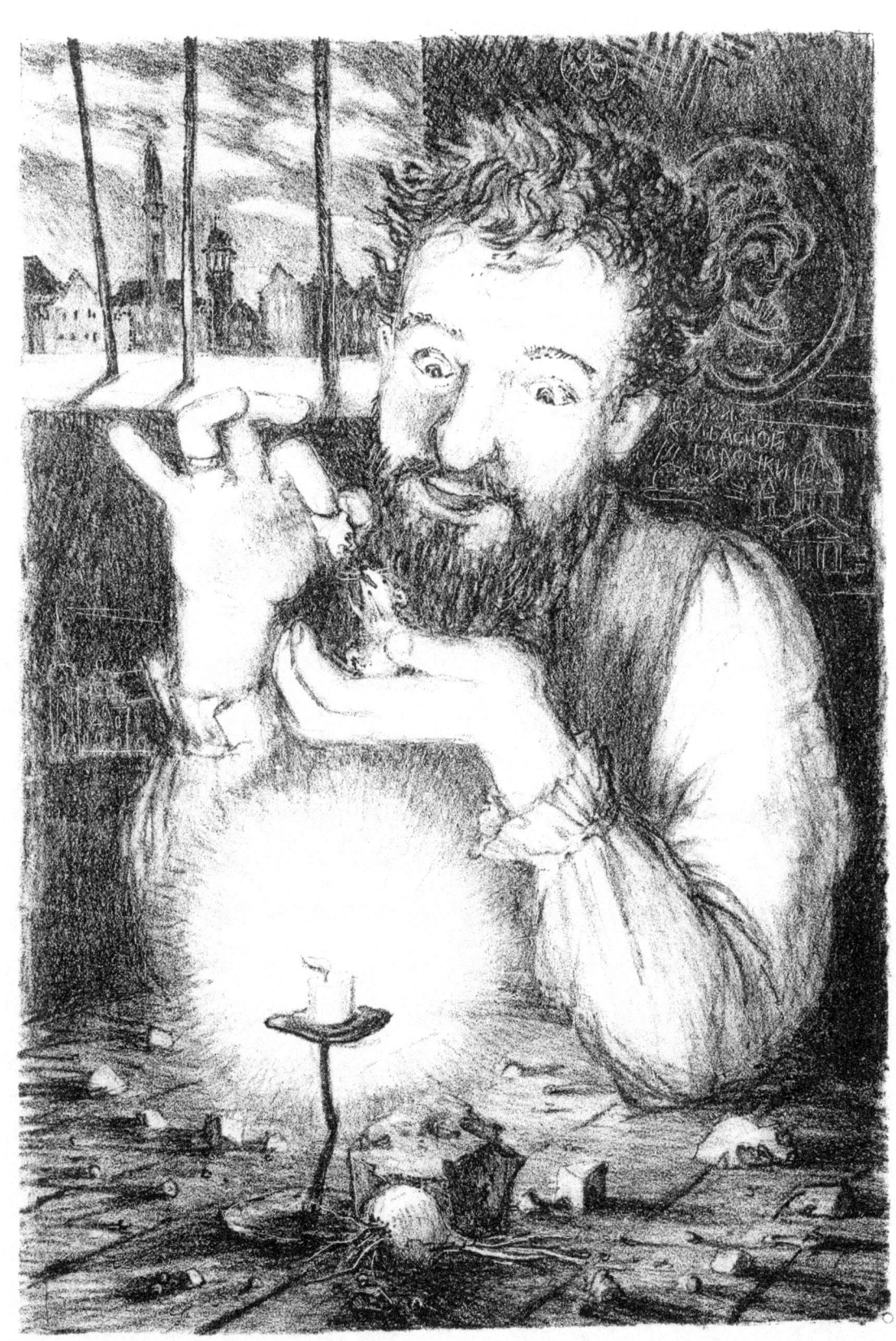

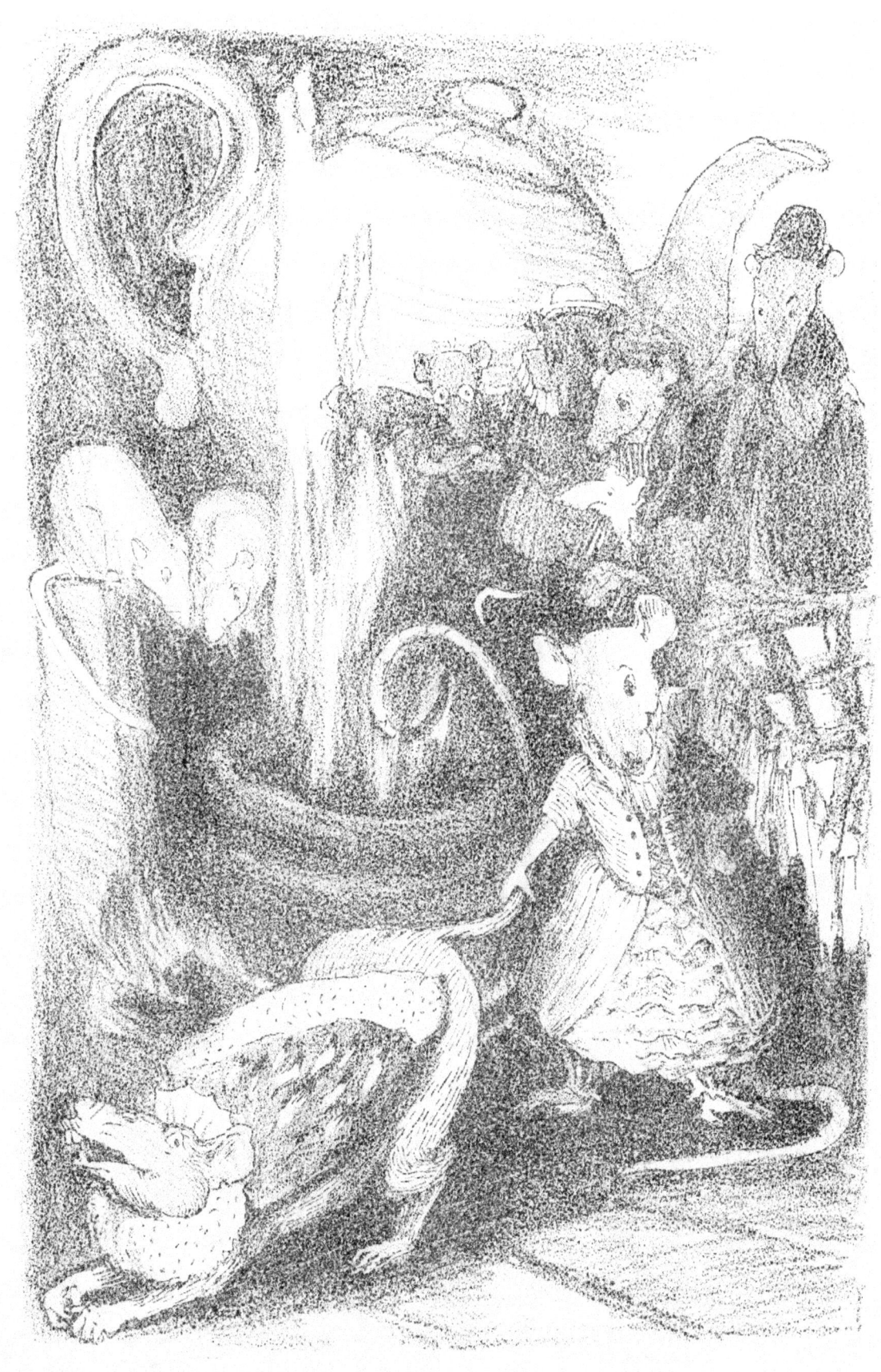

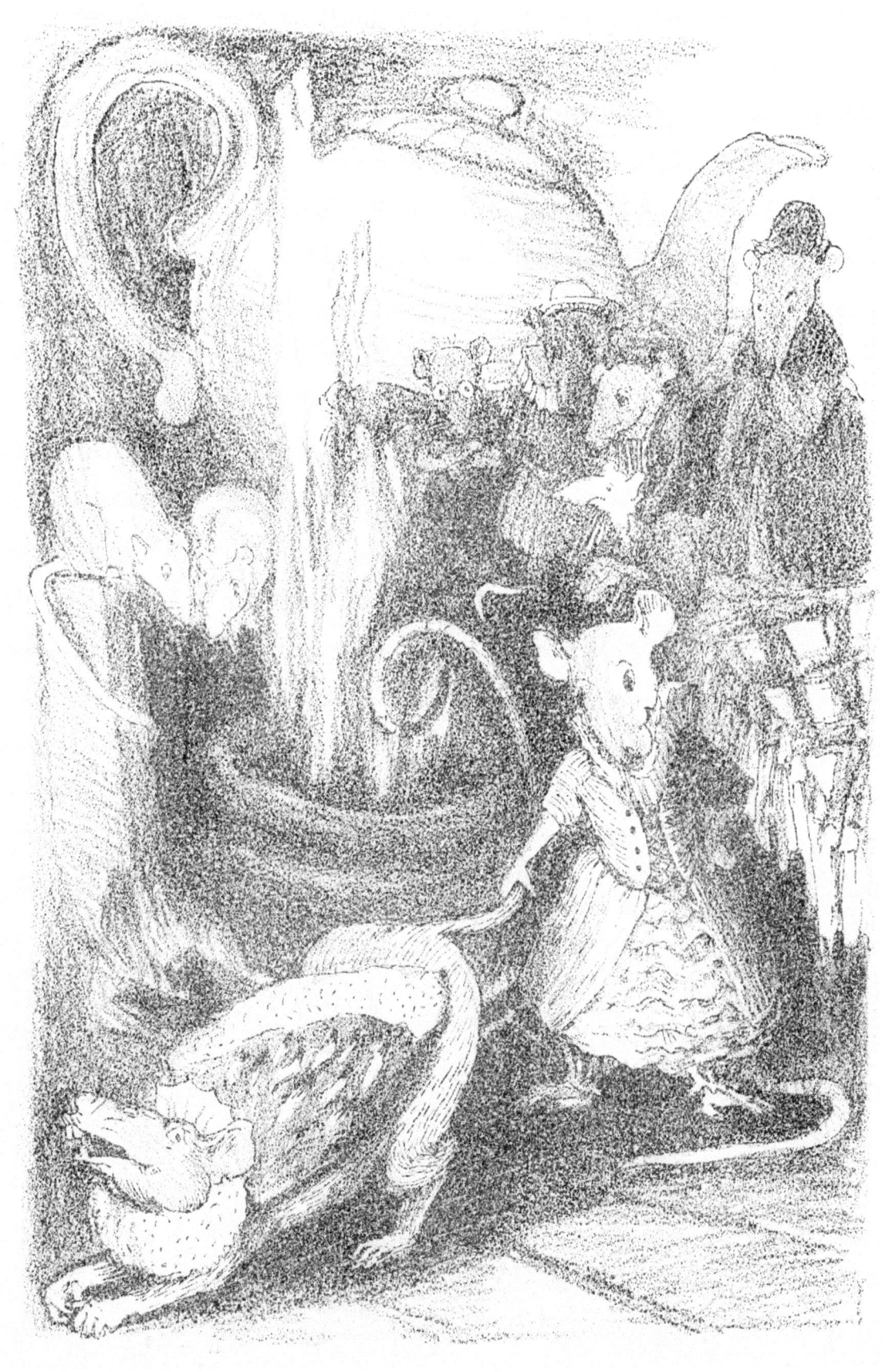

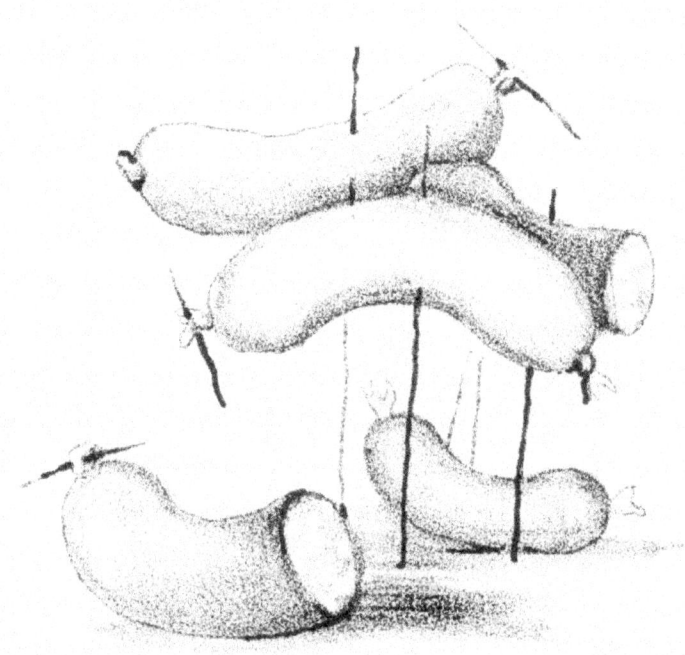

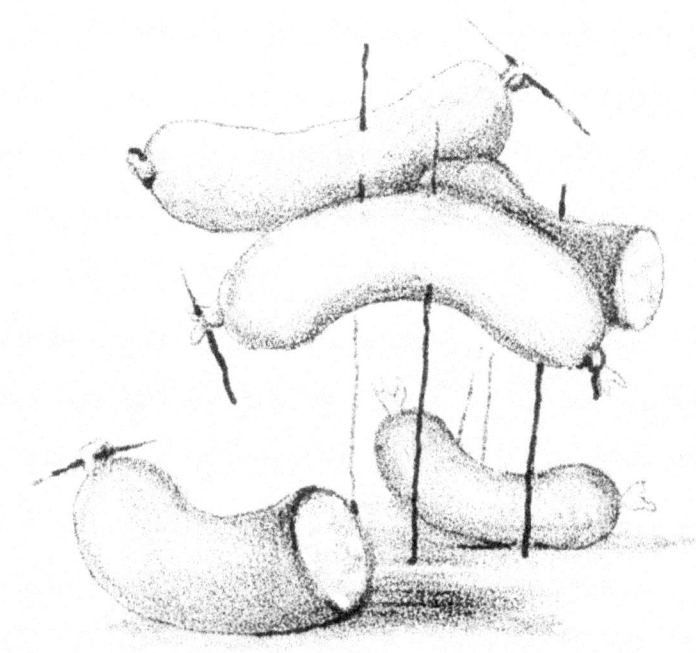

Little Ida's Flowers

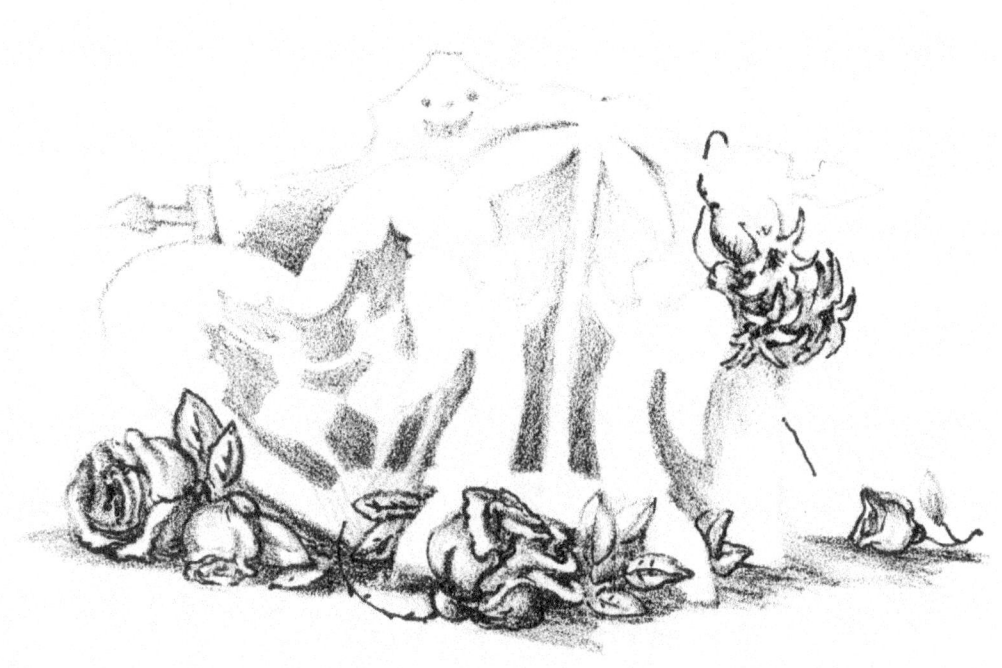

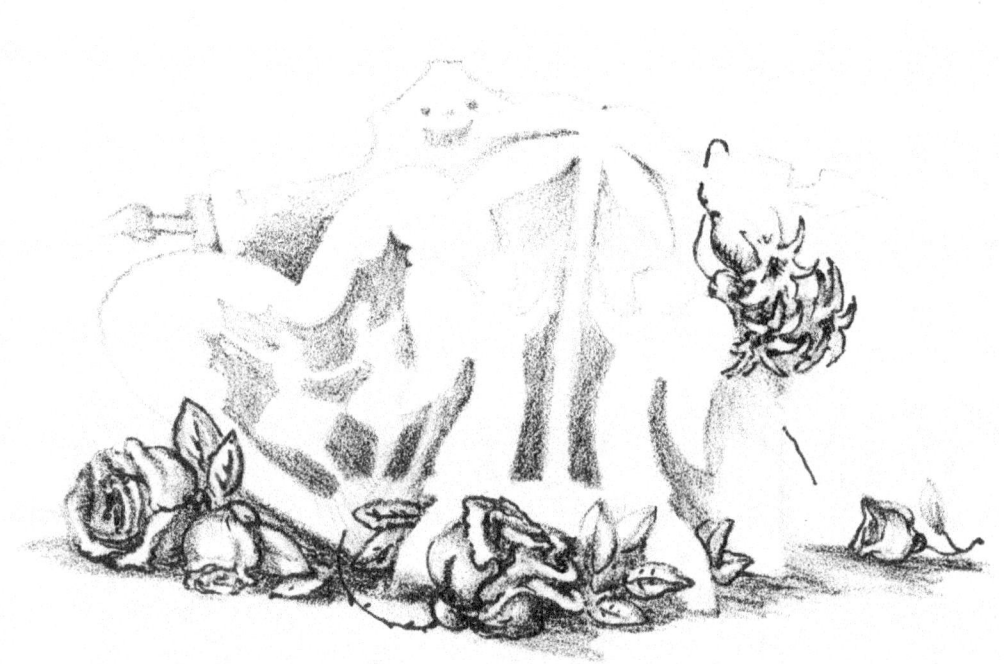

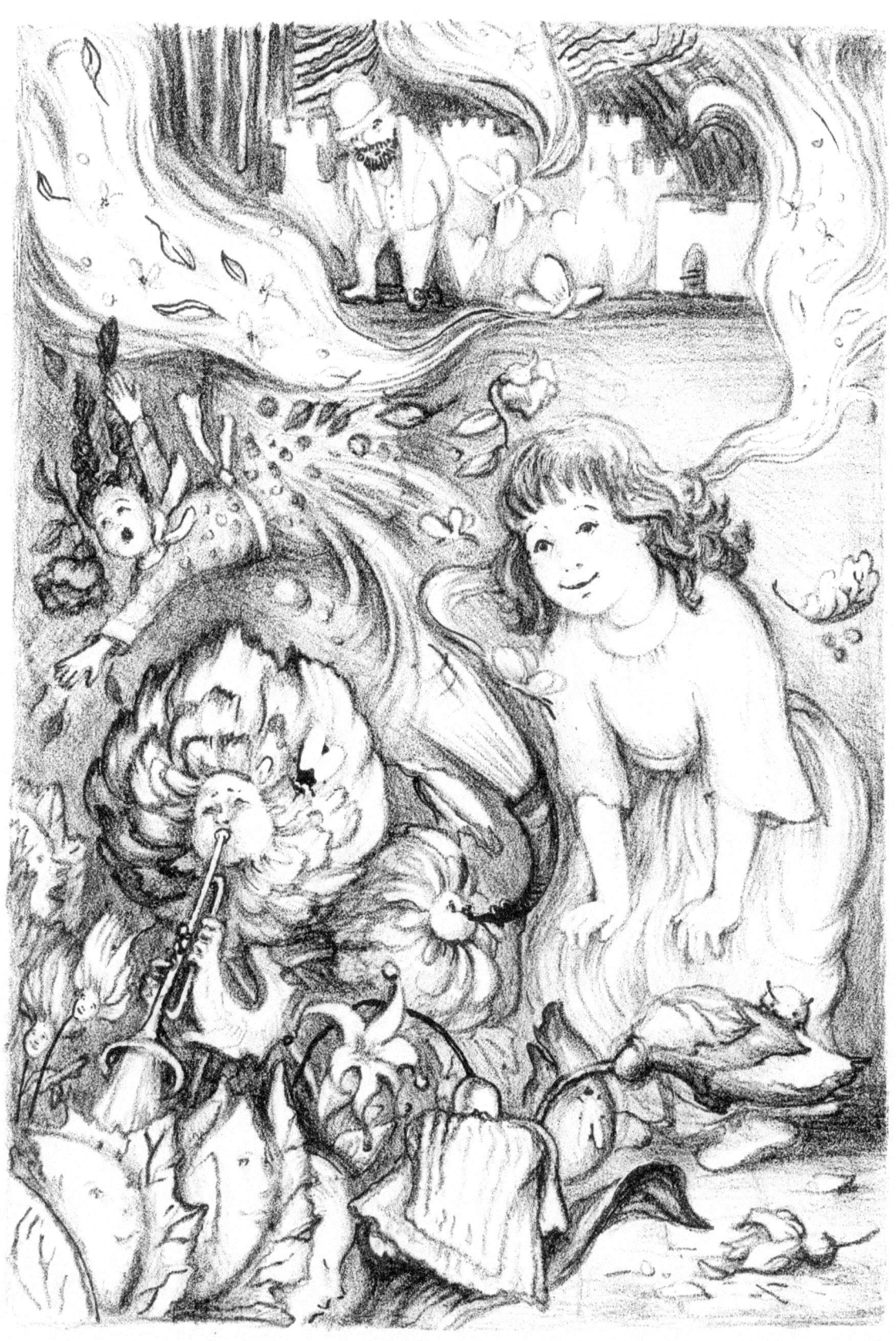

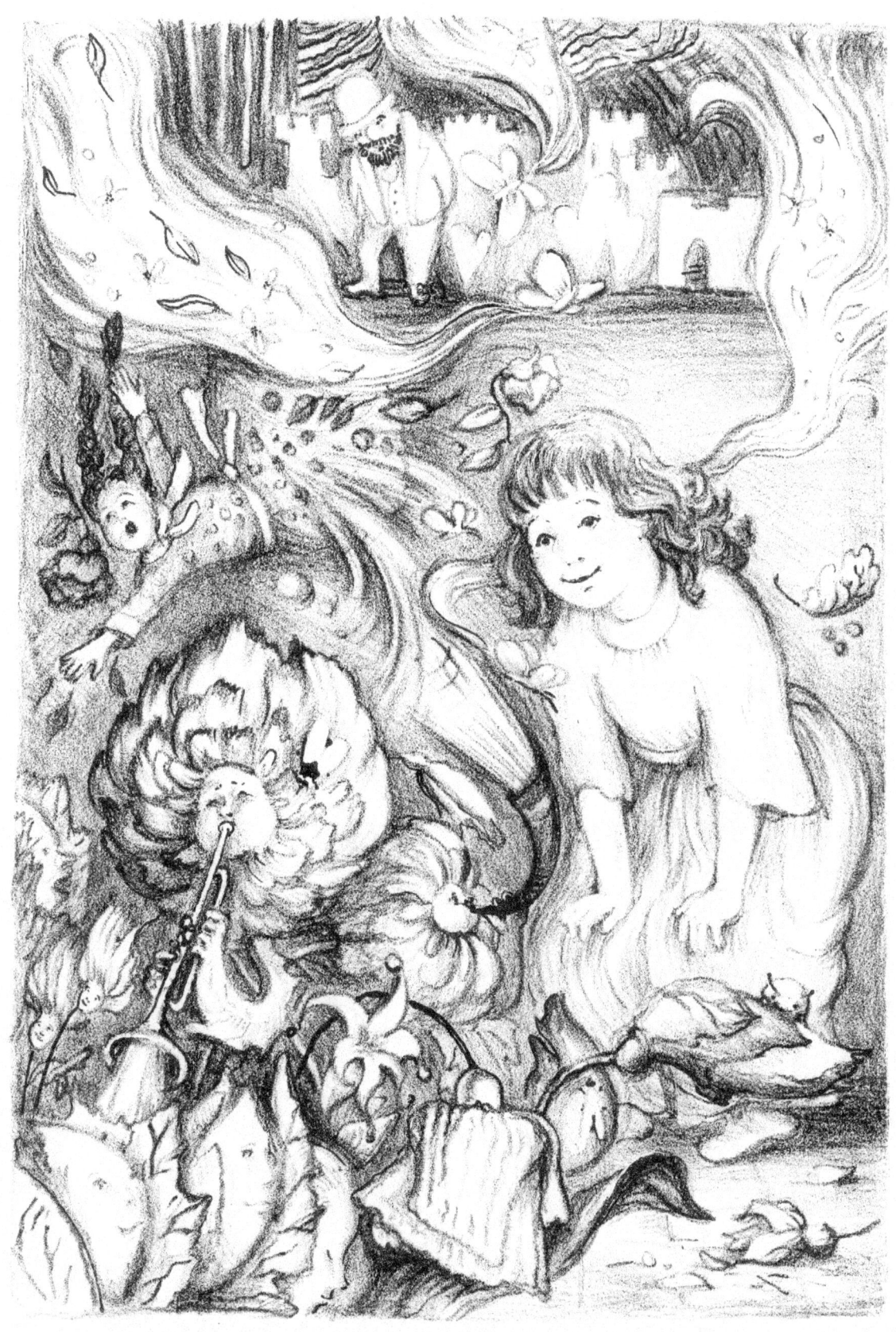

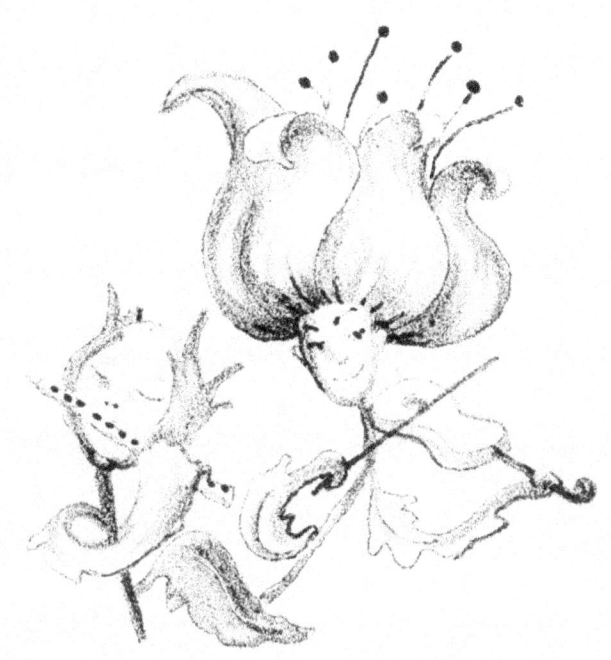

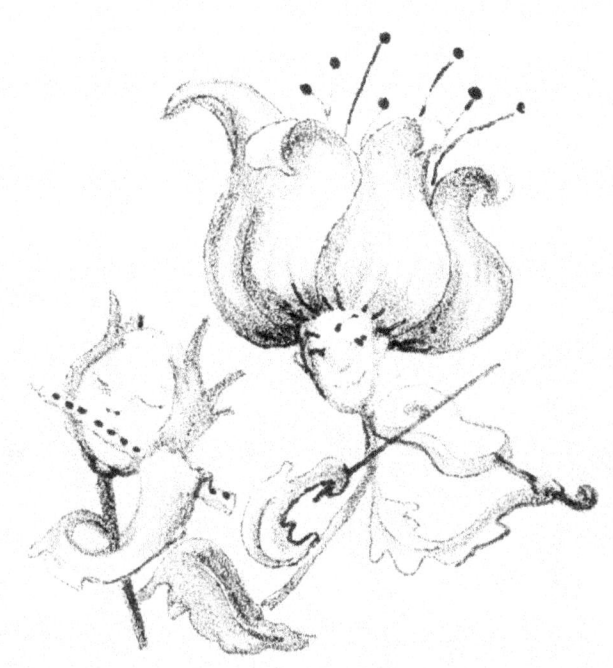

Little Claus
and
Big Claus

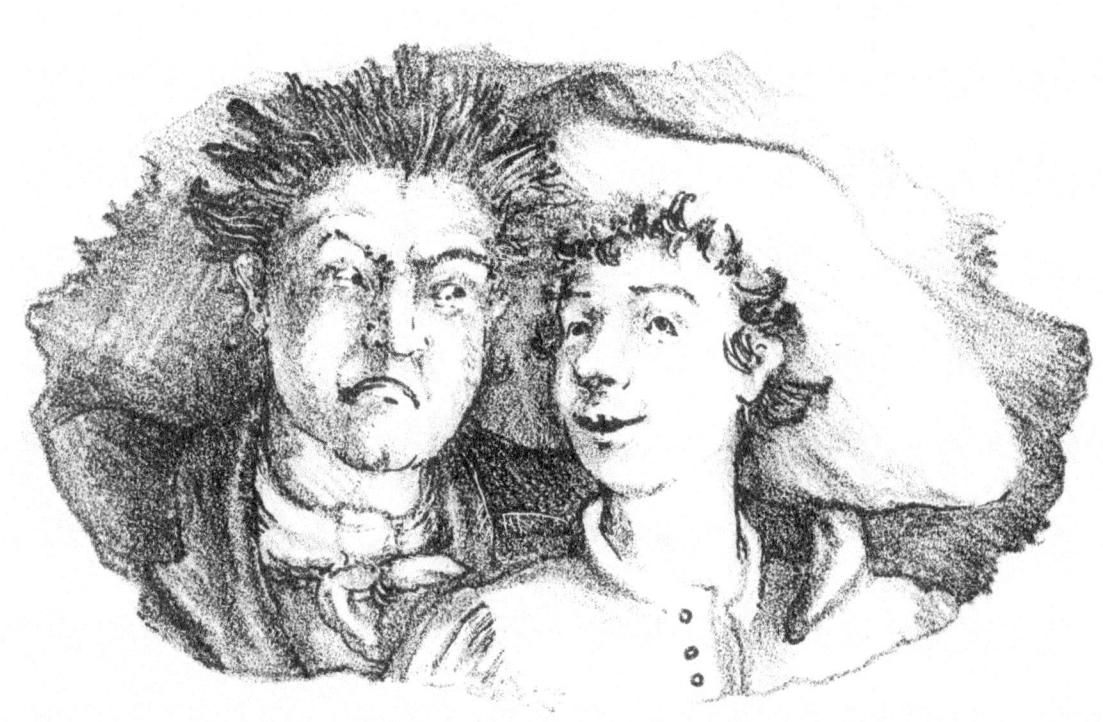

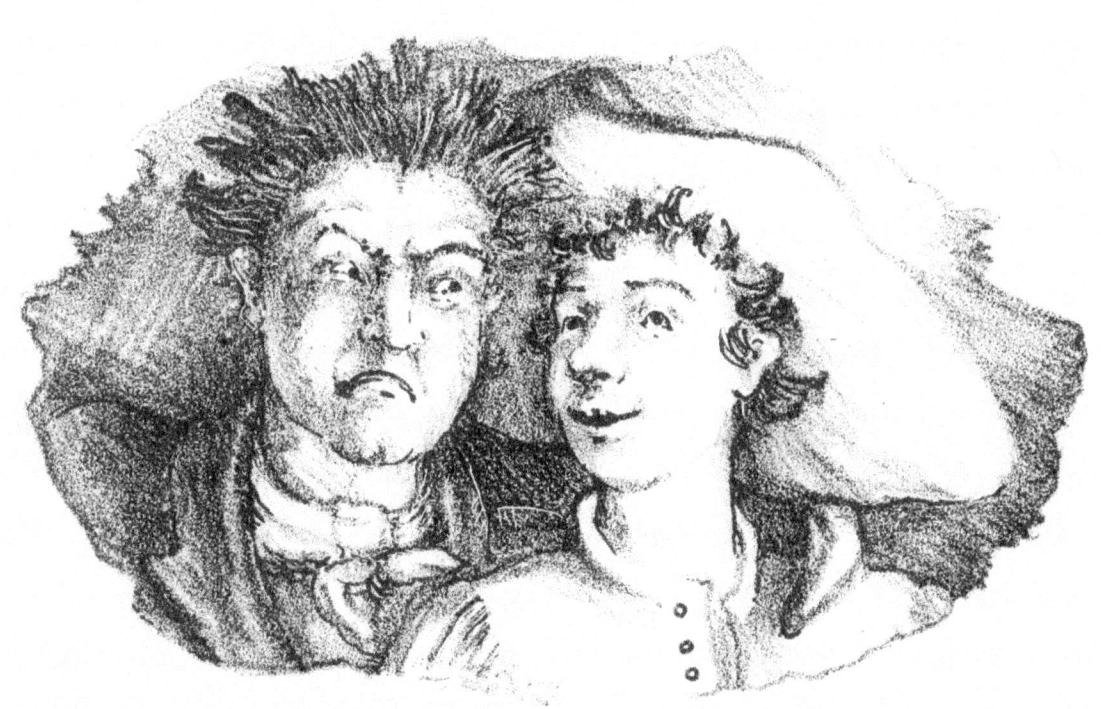

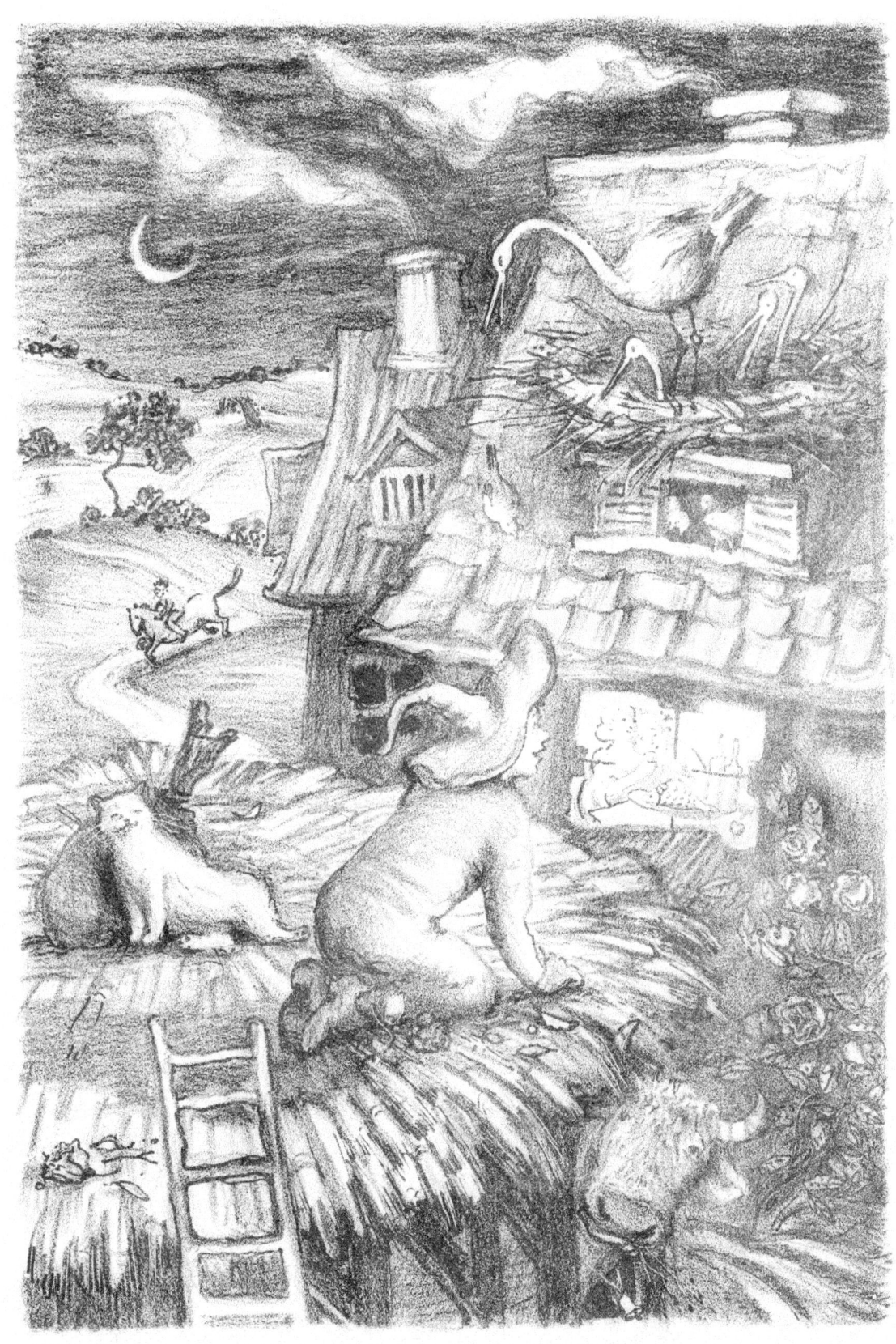

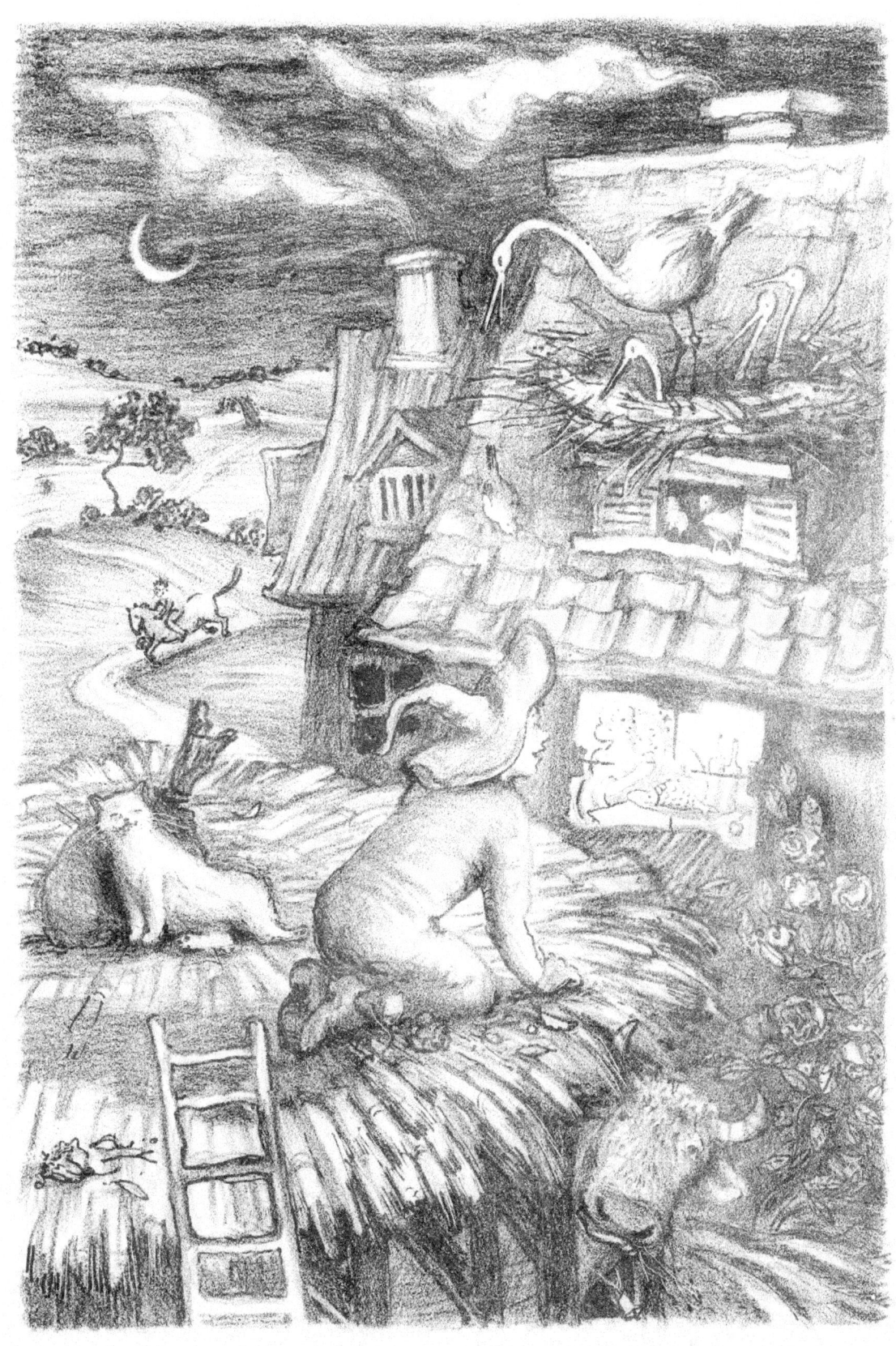

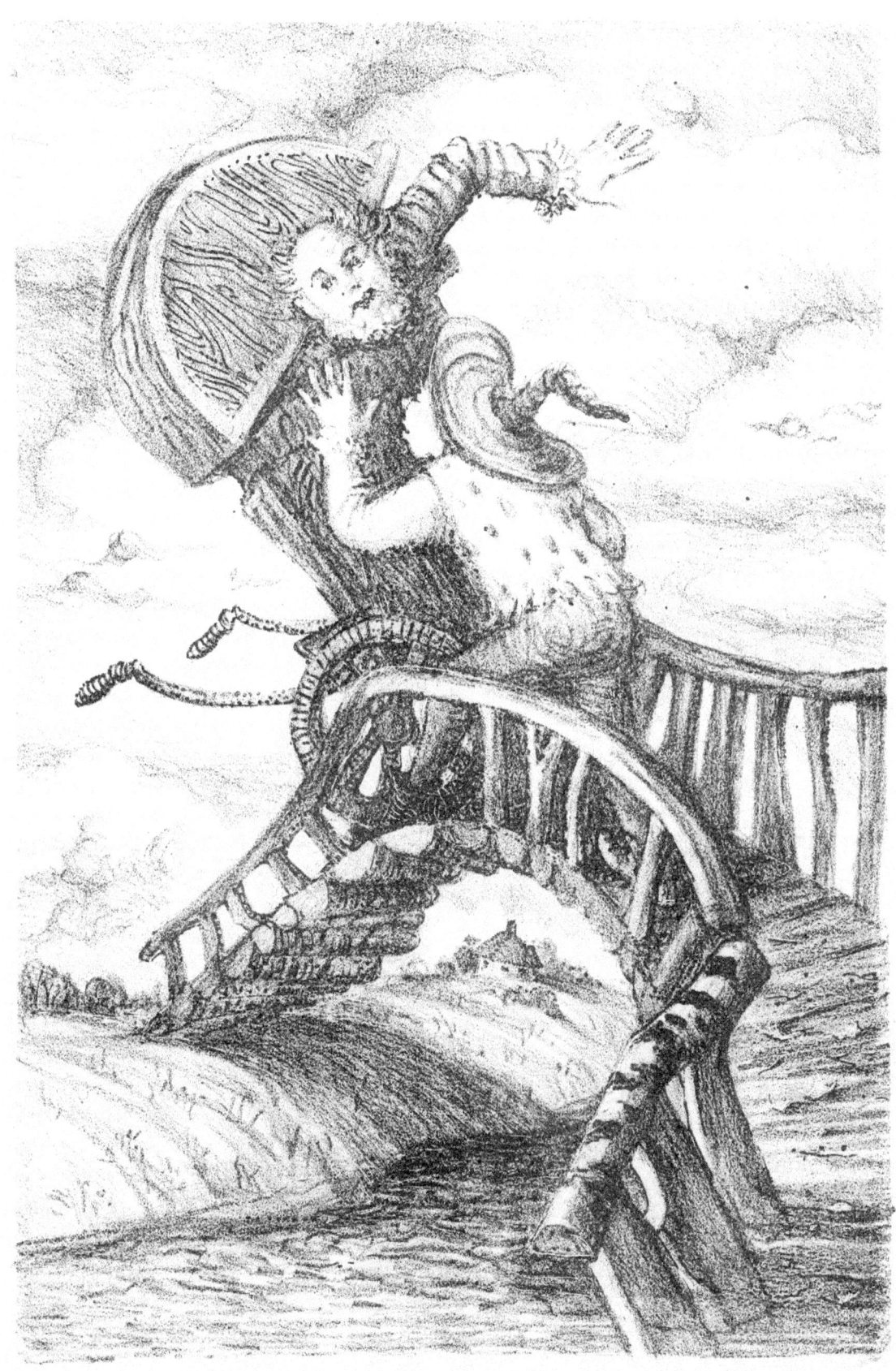

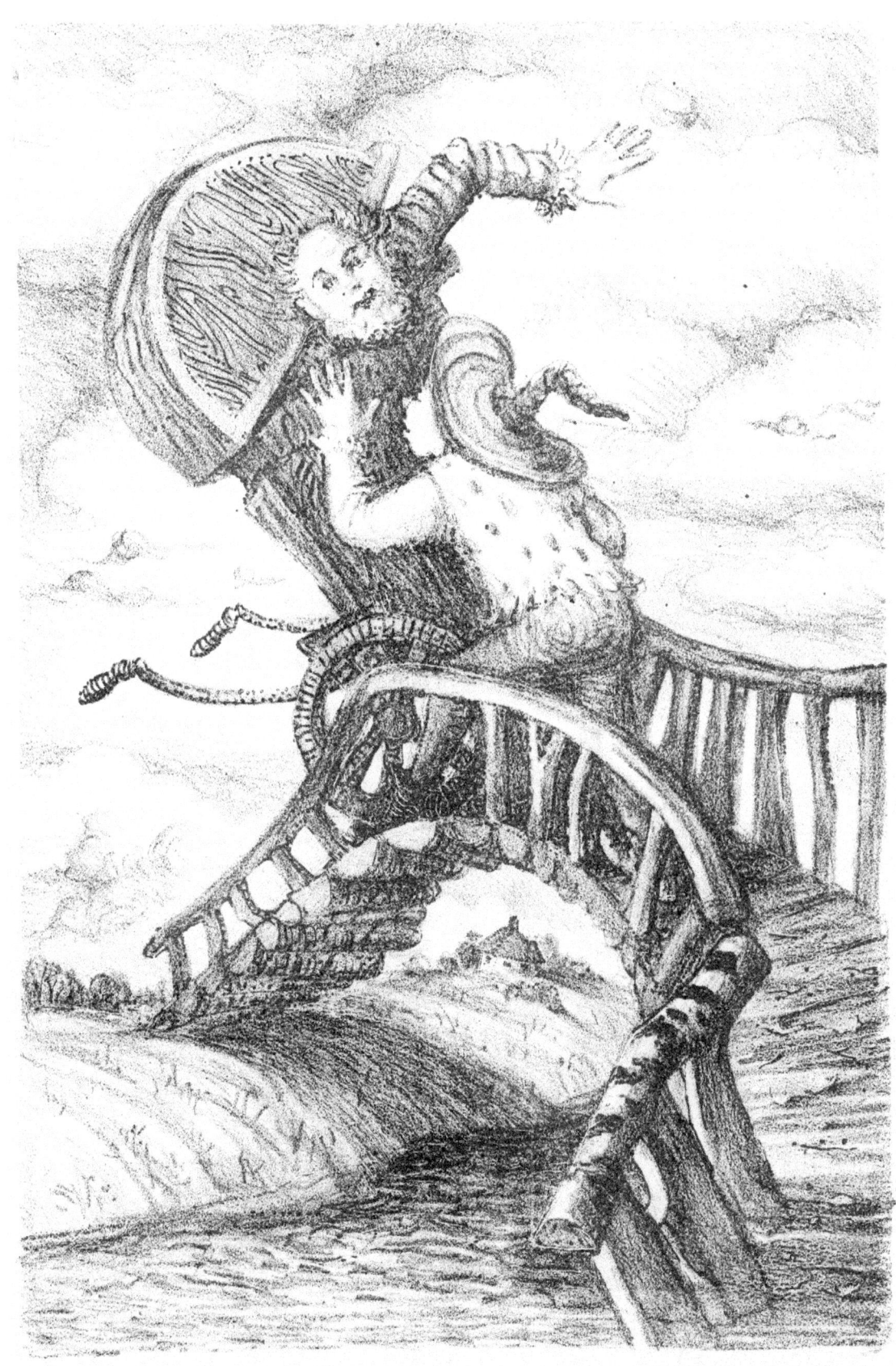

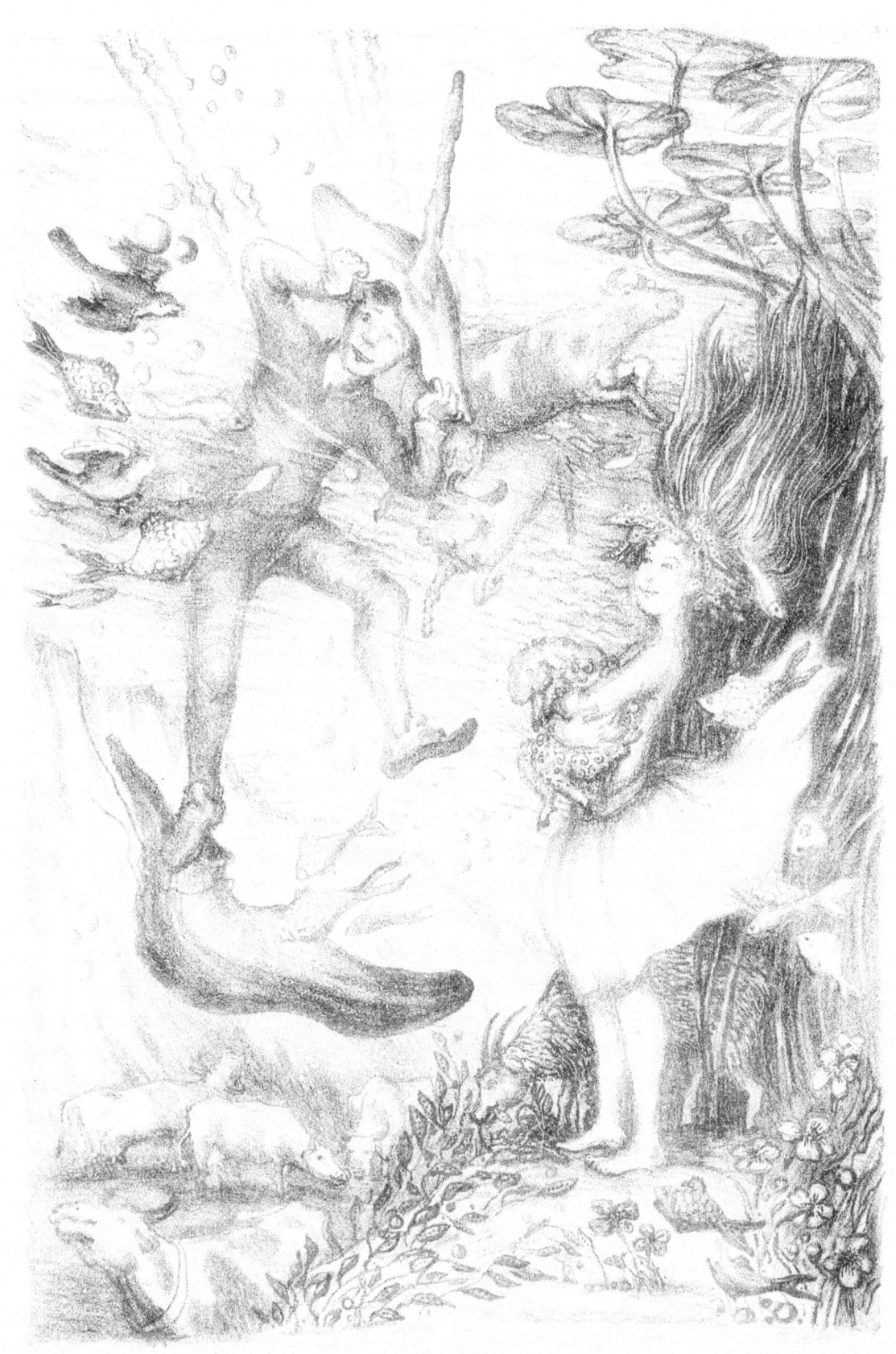

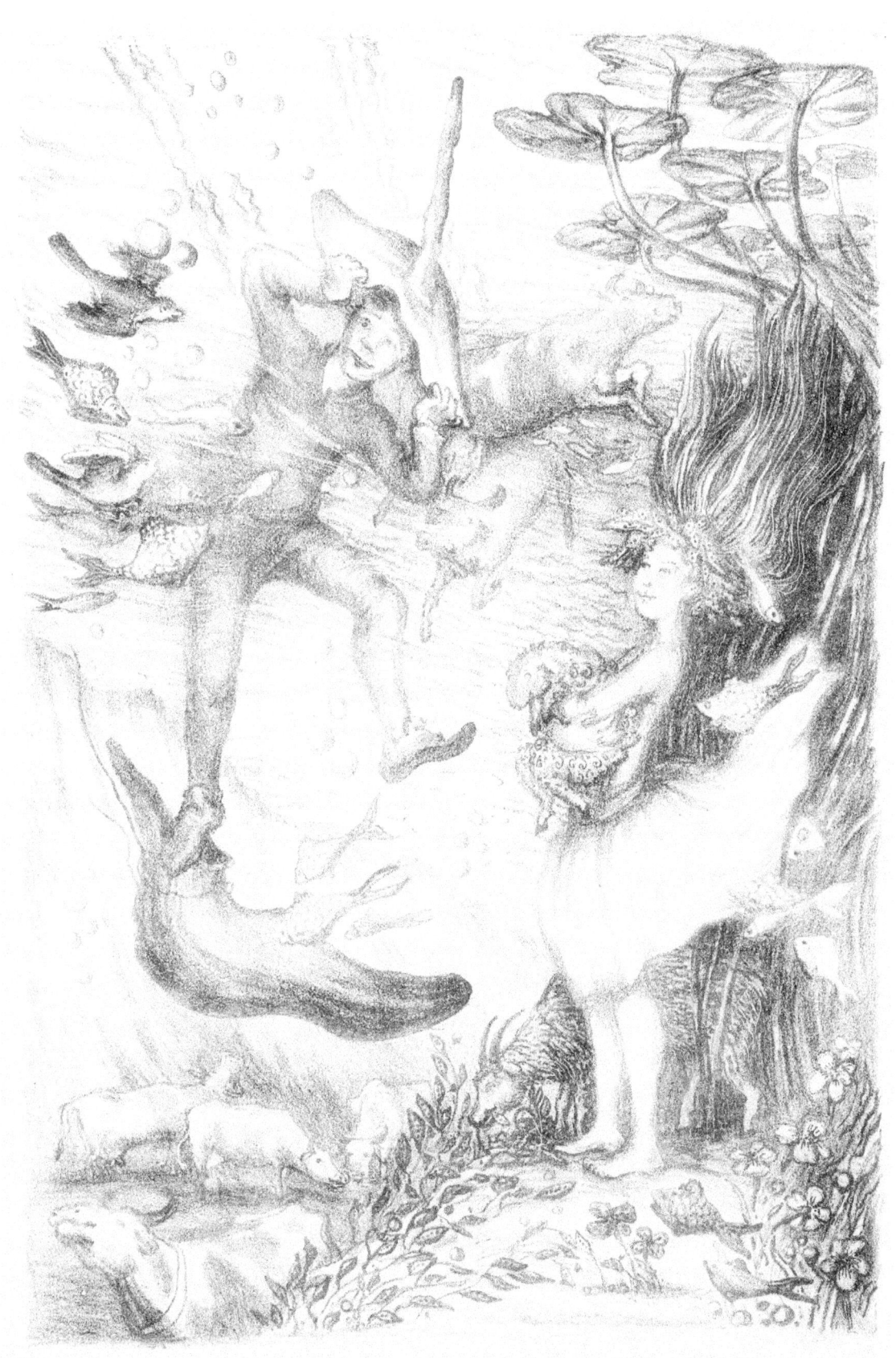

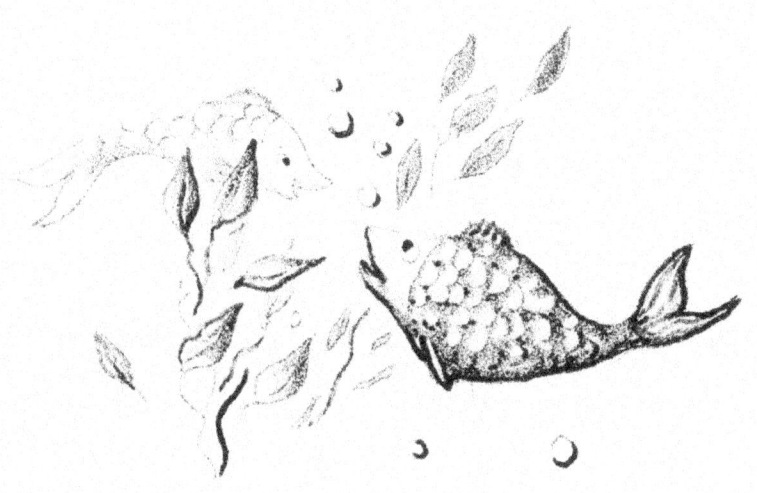

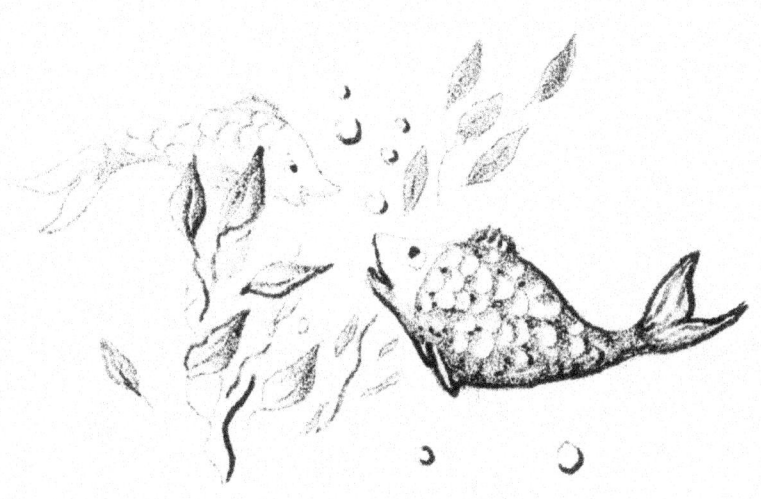

Ole Lukoie

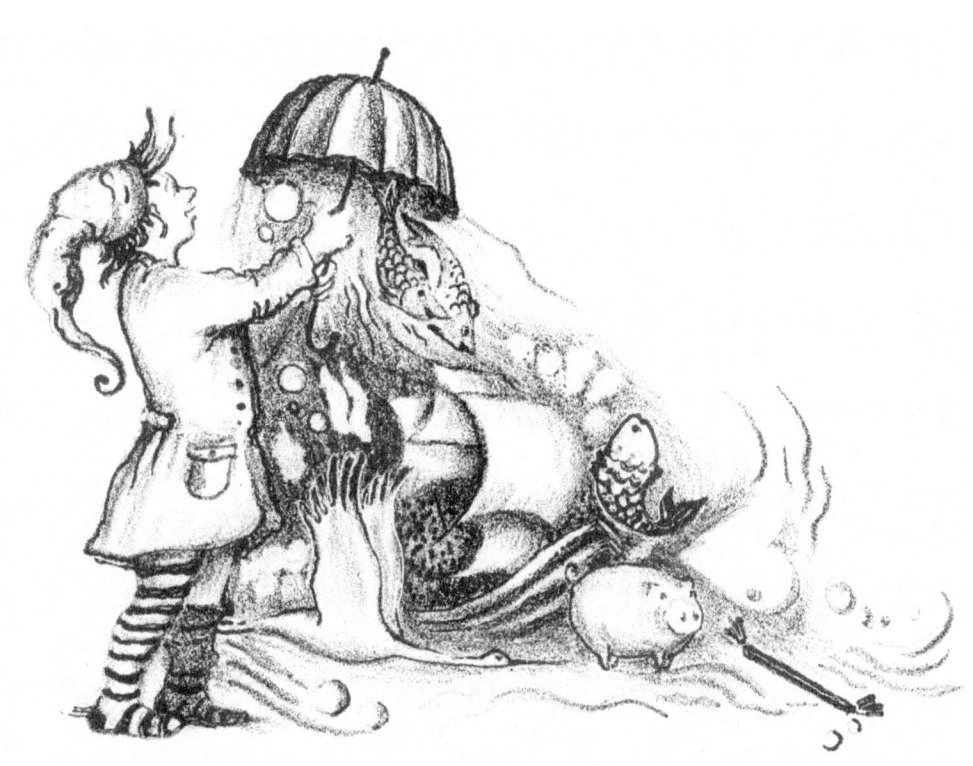

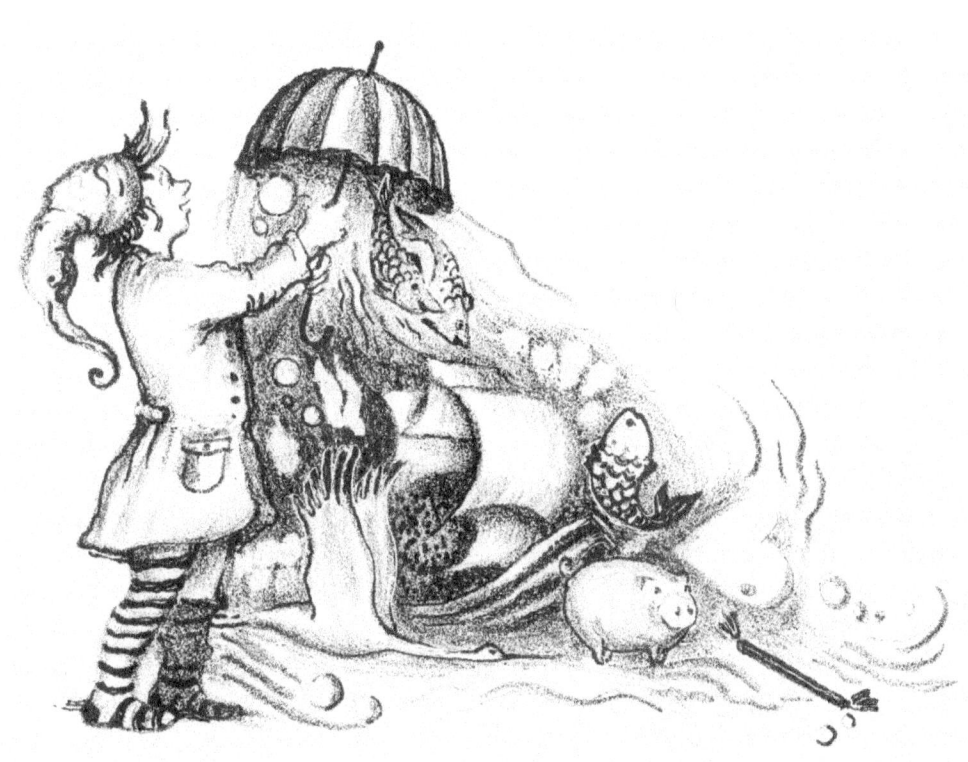

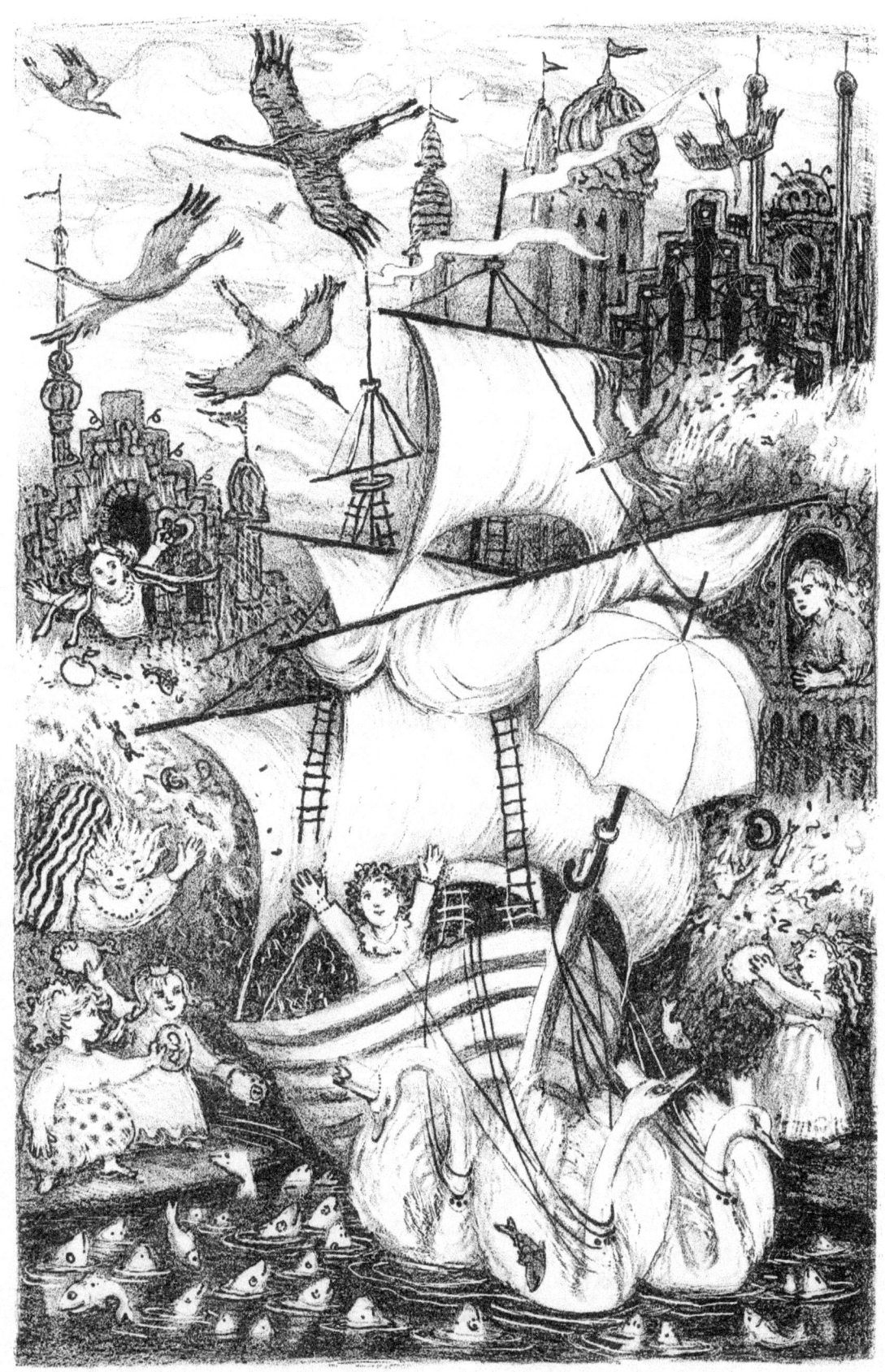

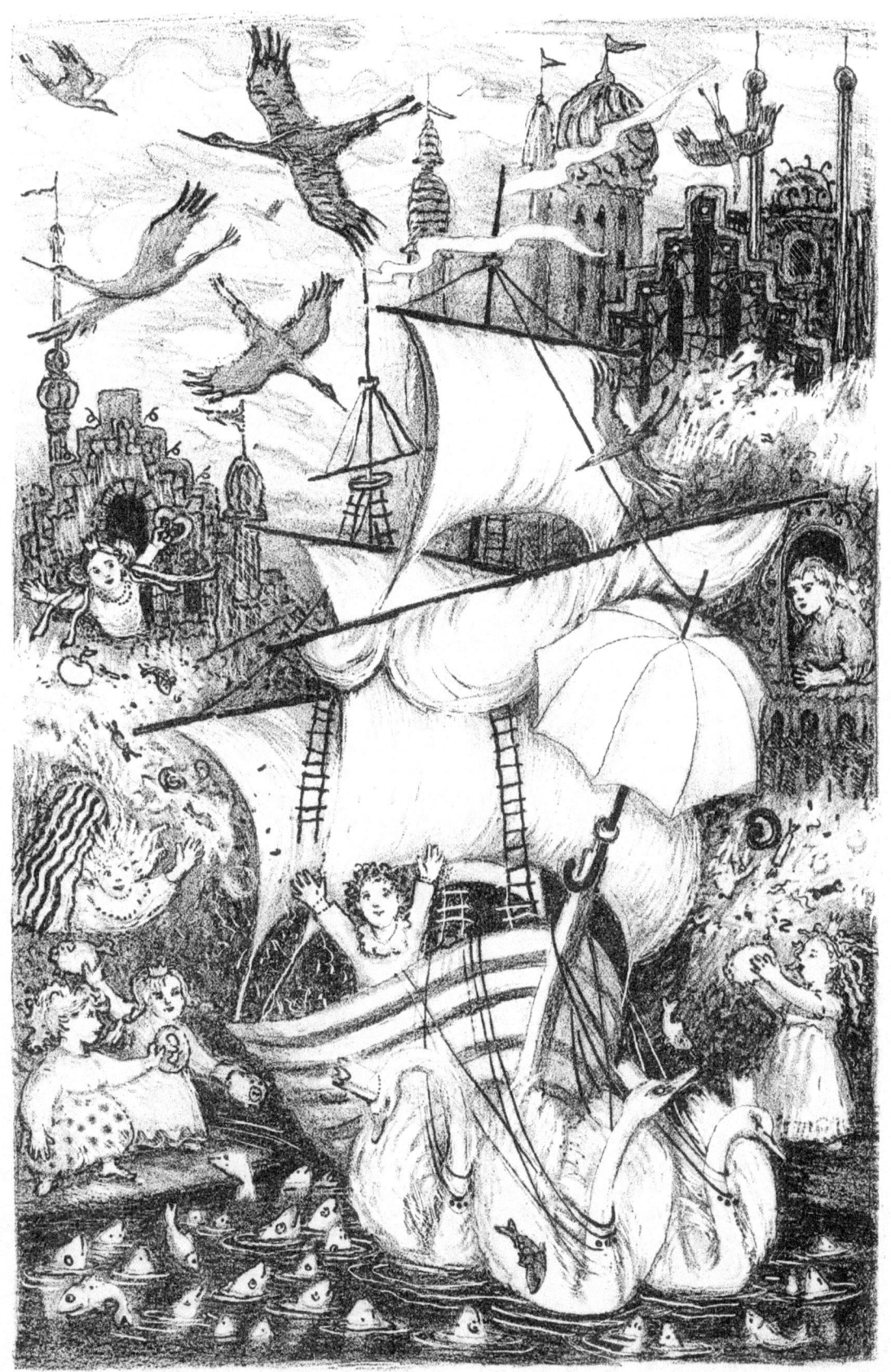

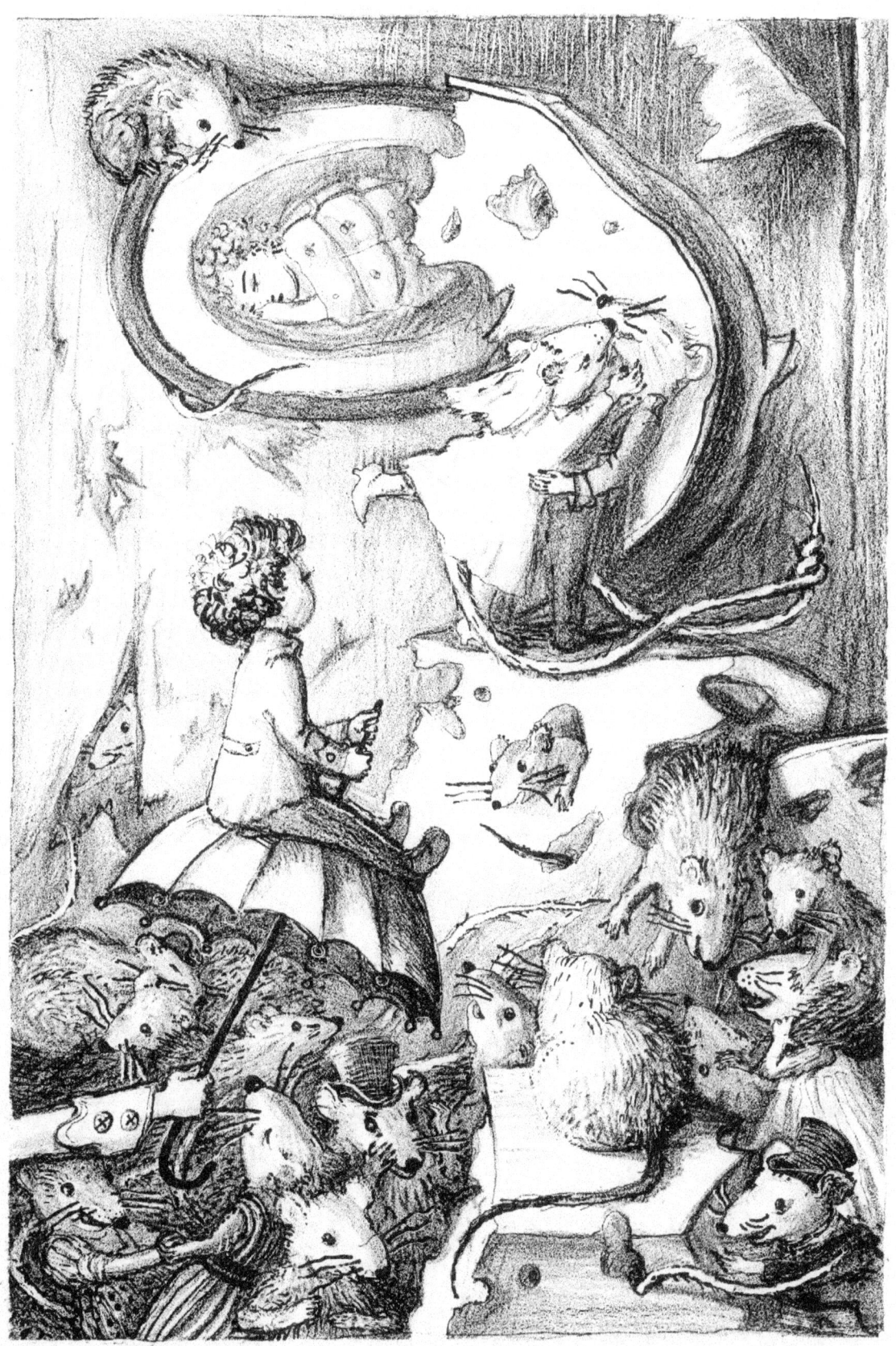

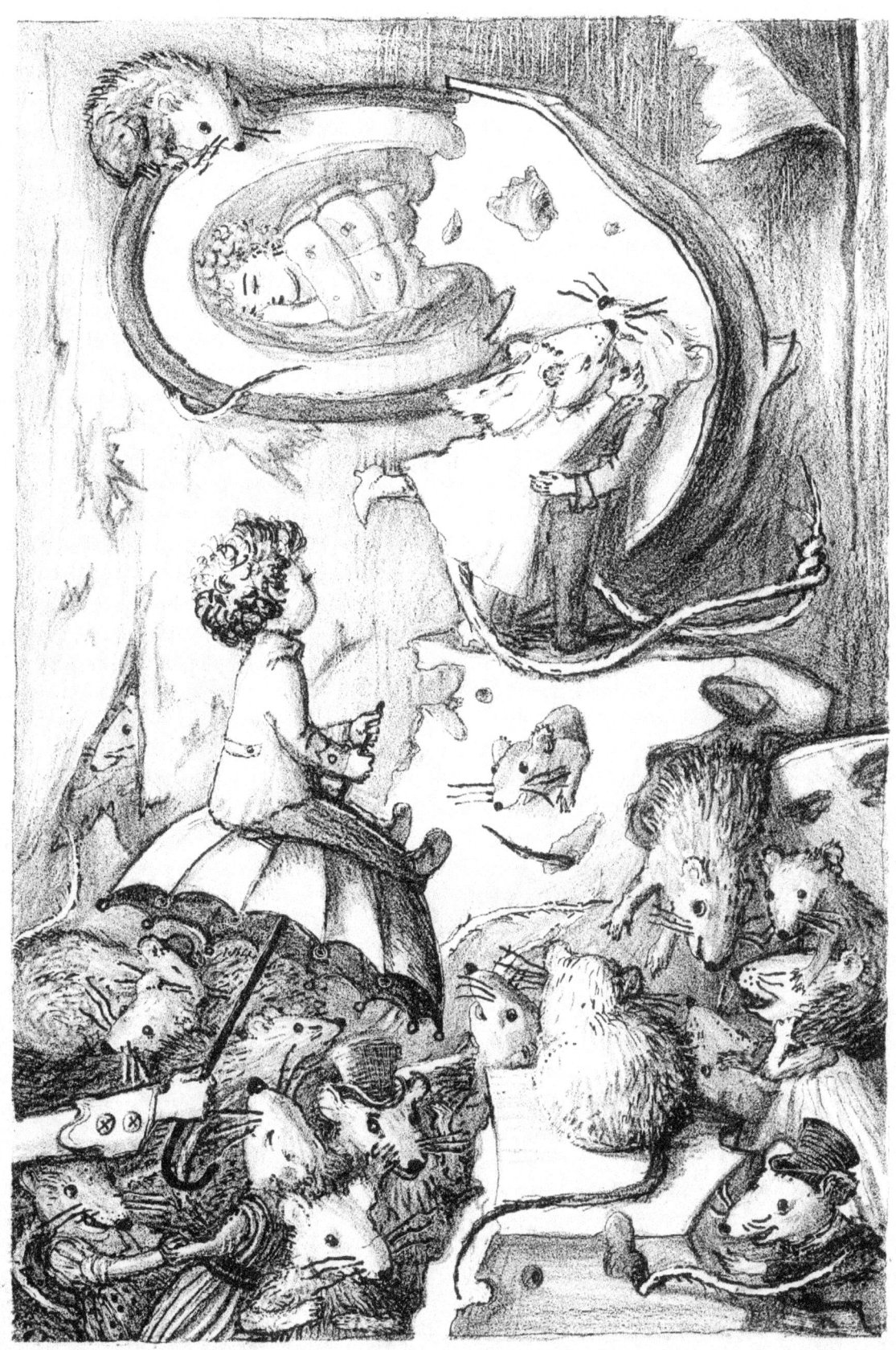

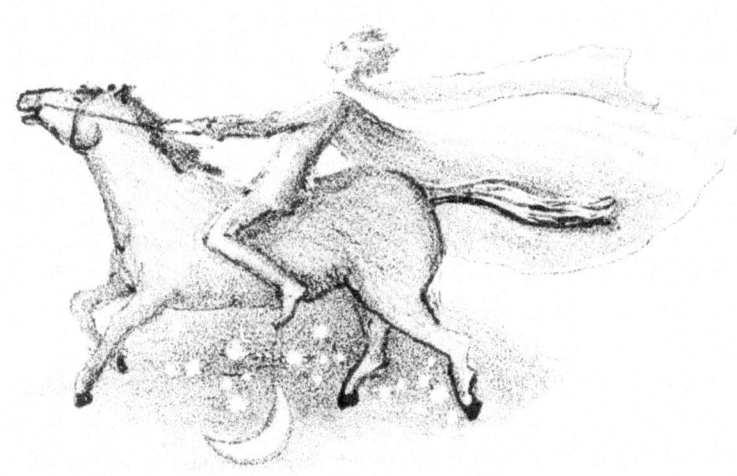

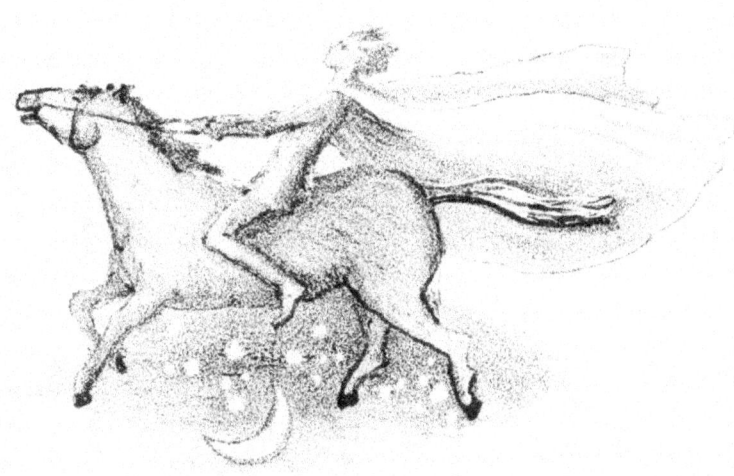

Ib

and Little

Christine

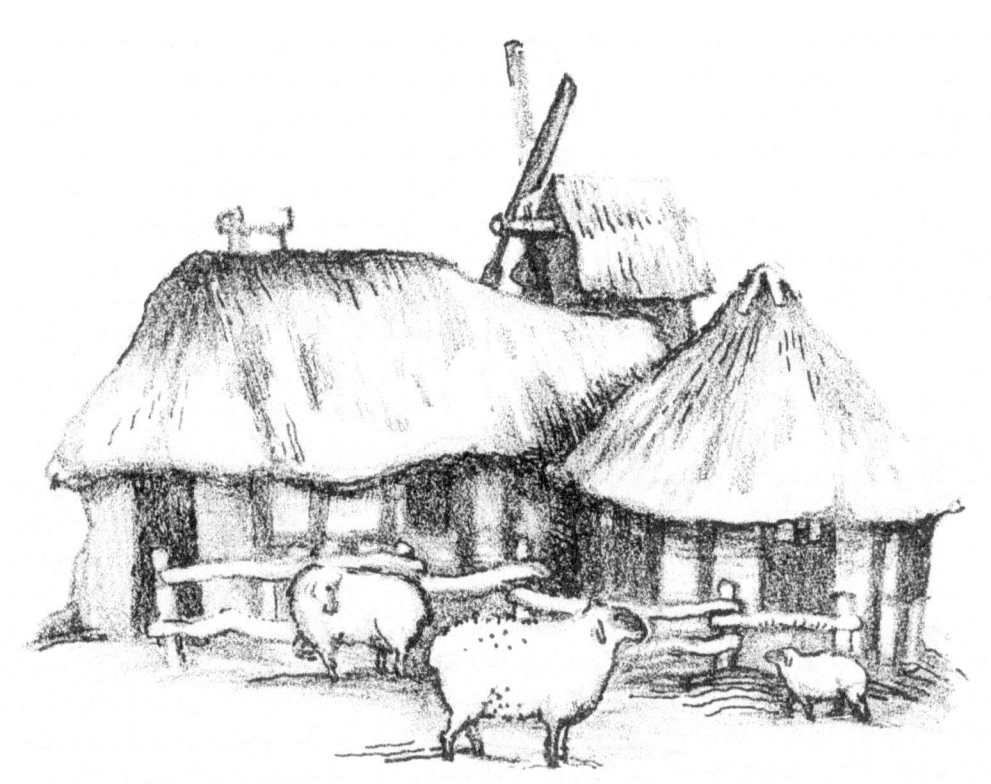

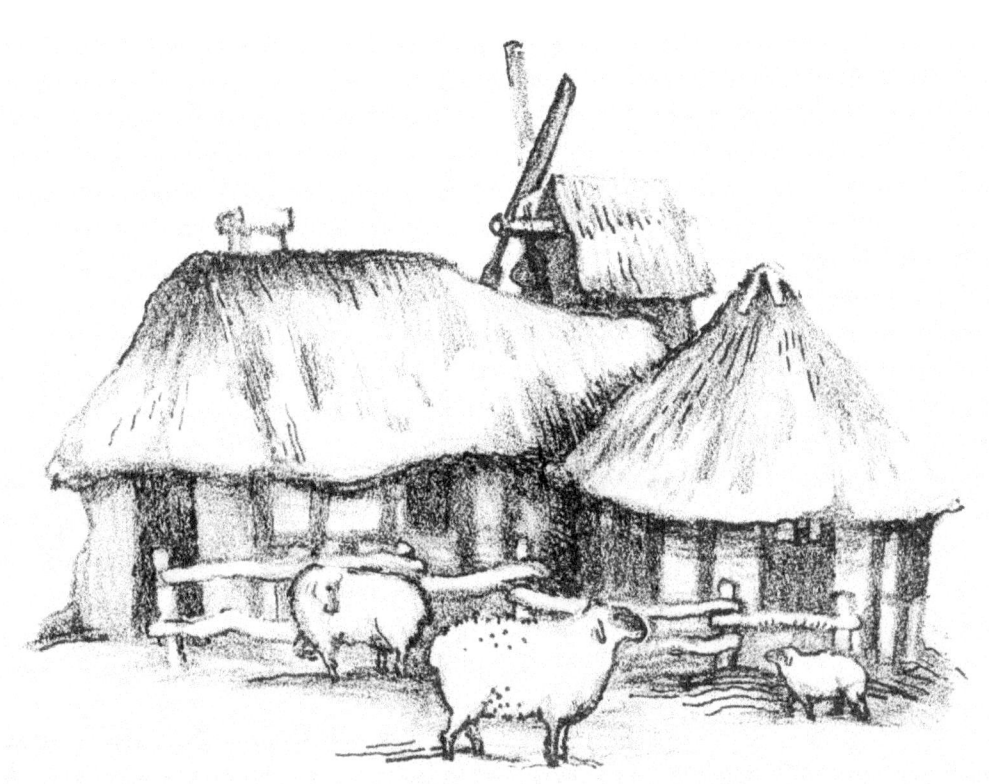

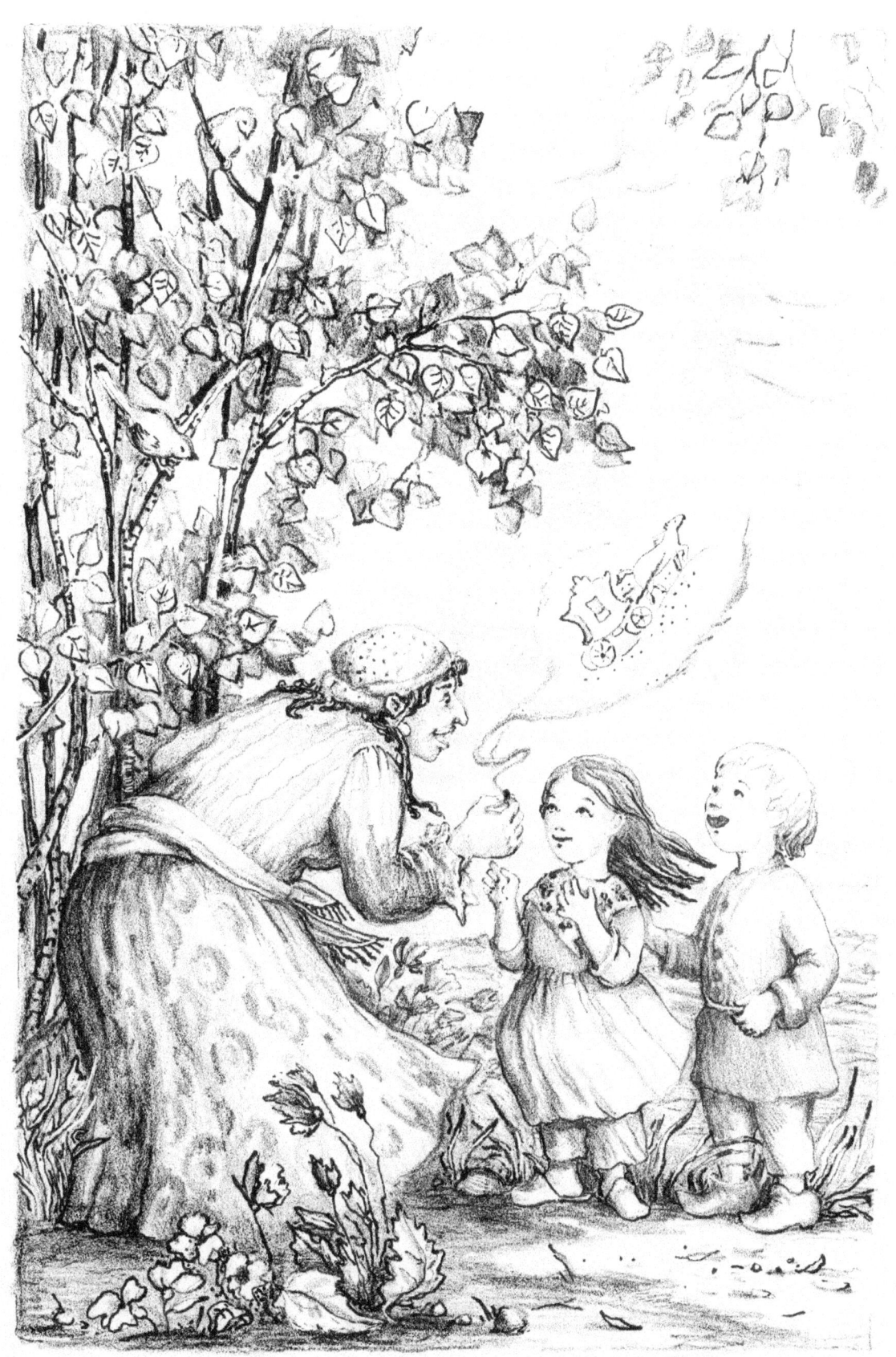

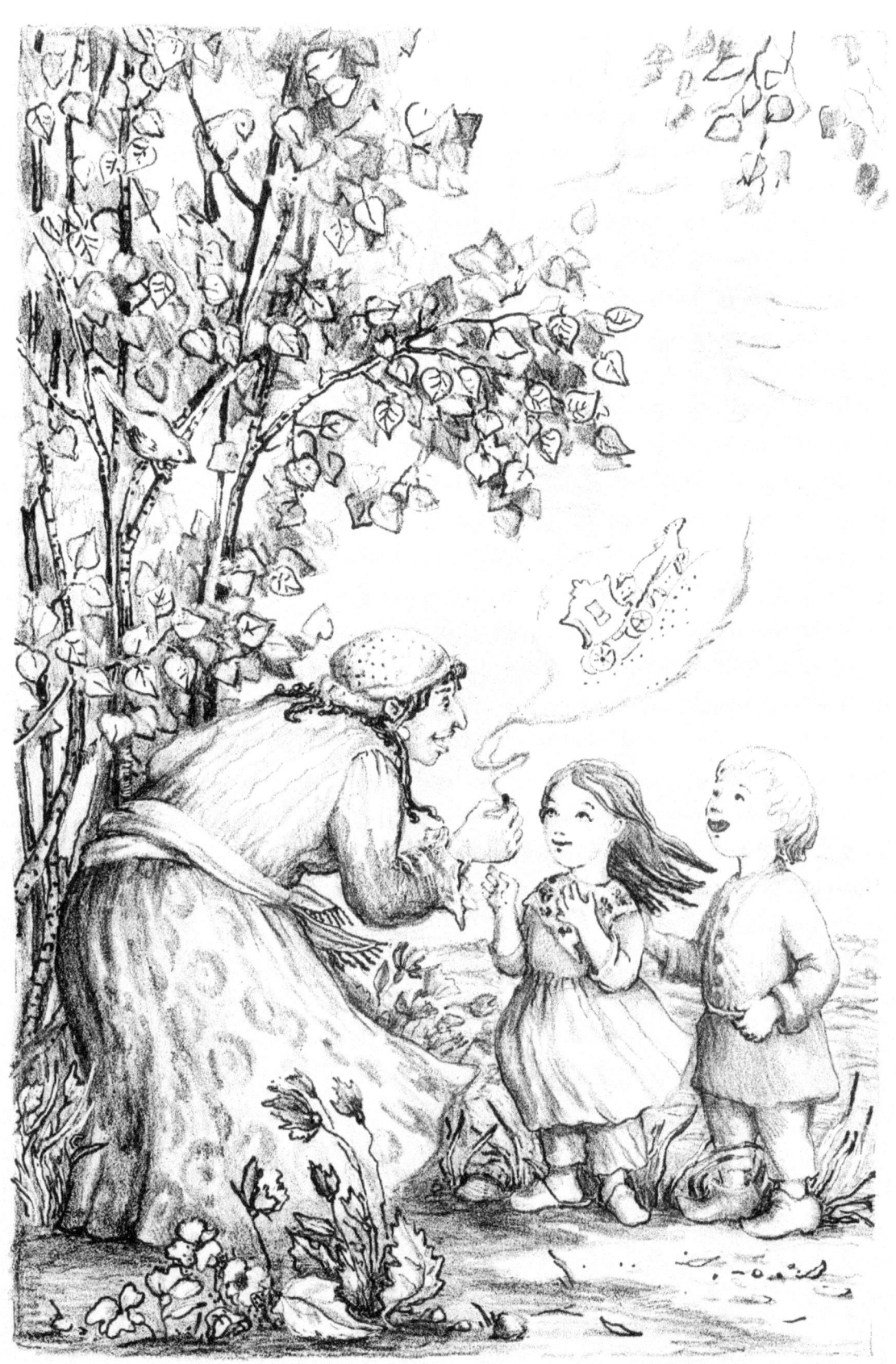

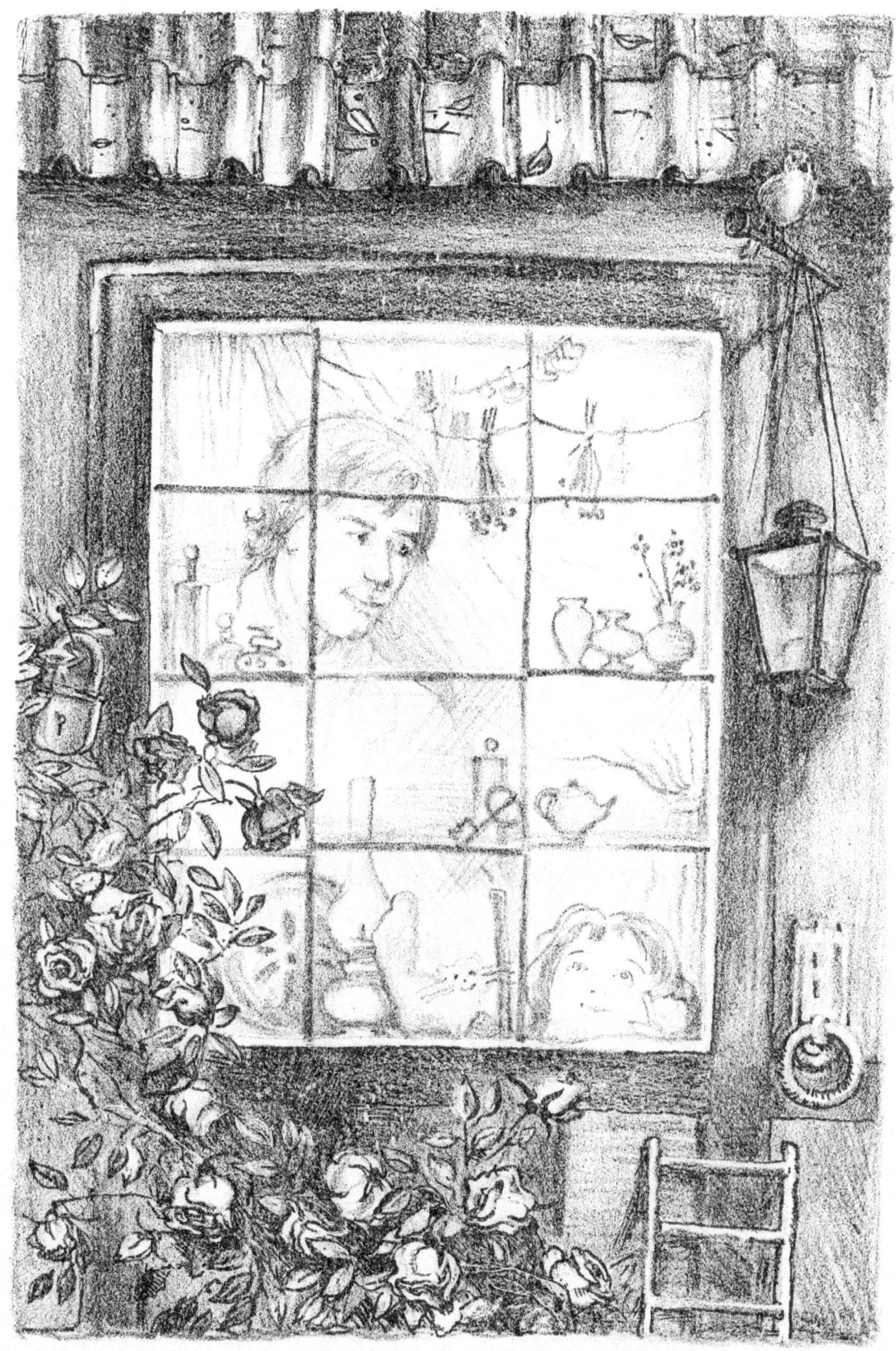

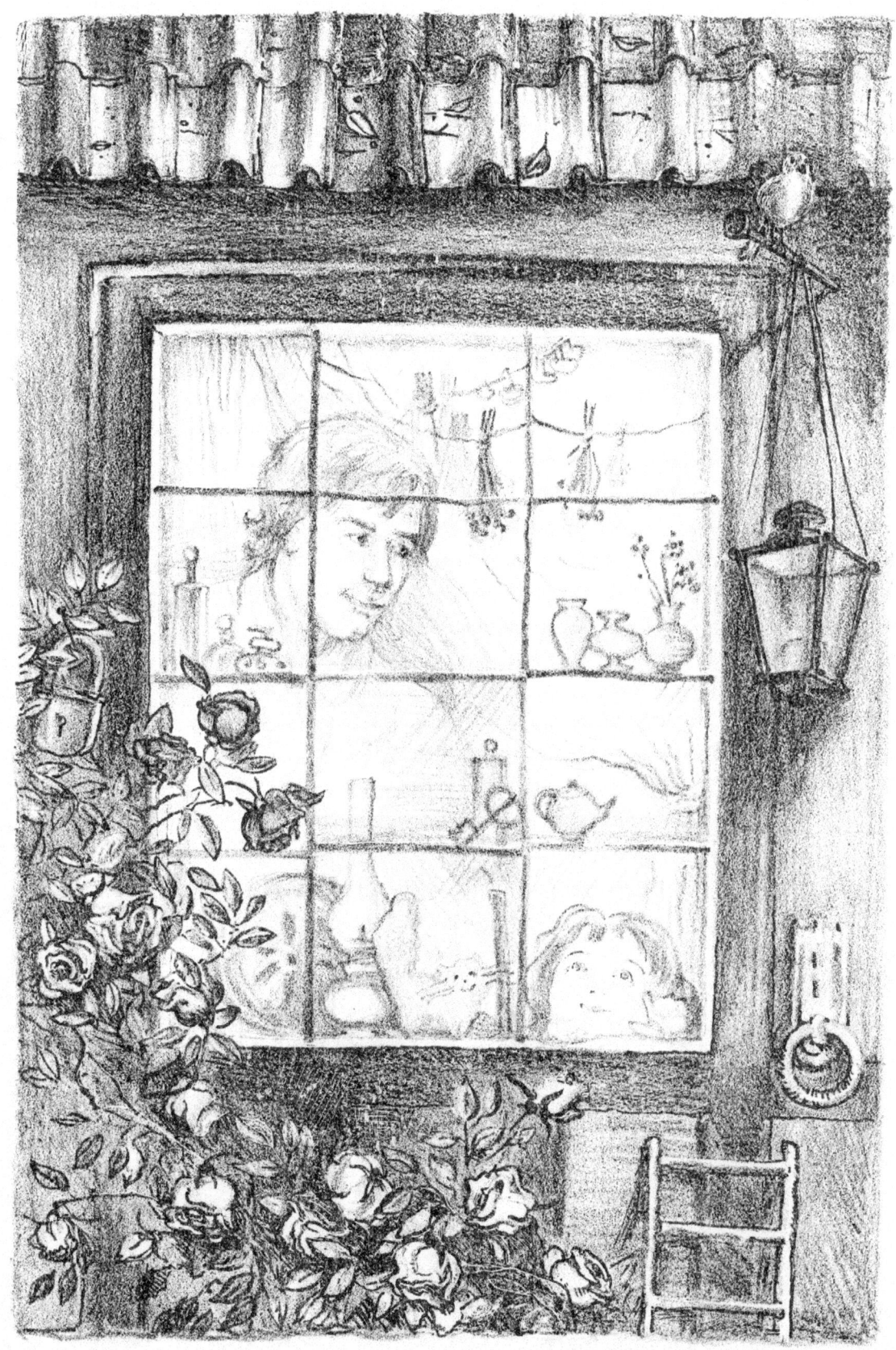

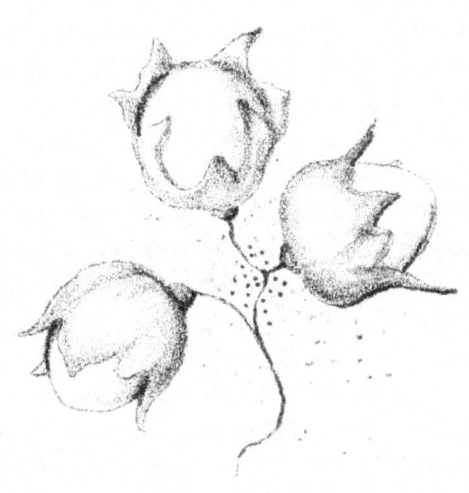

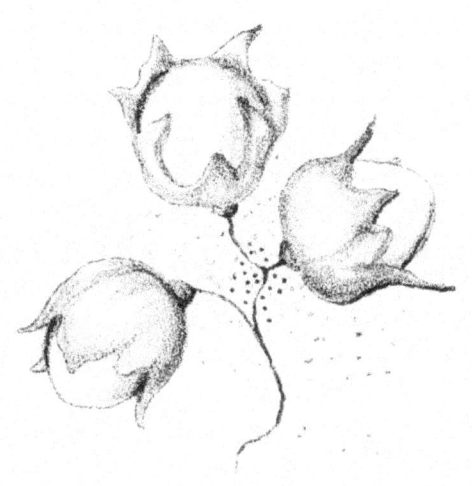

The Elf Mound

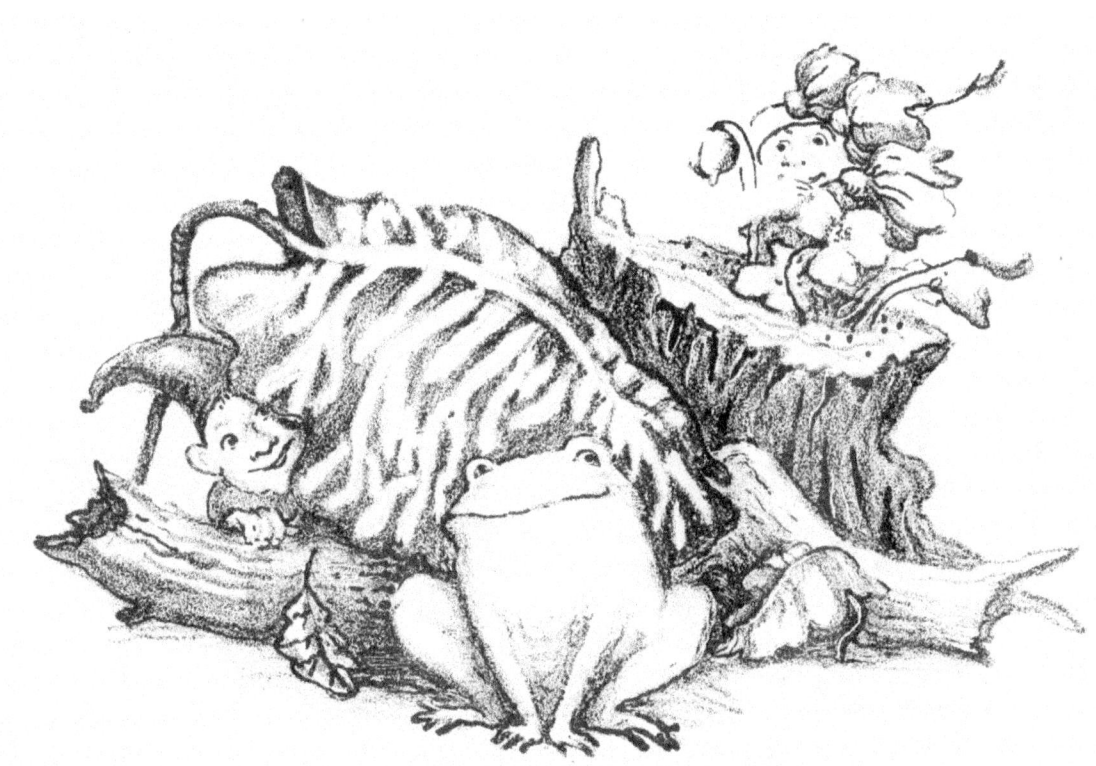

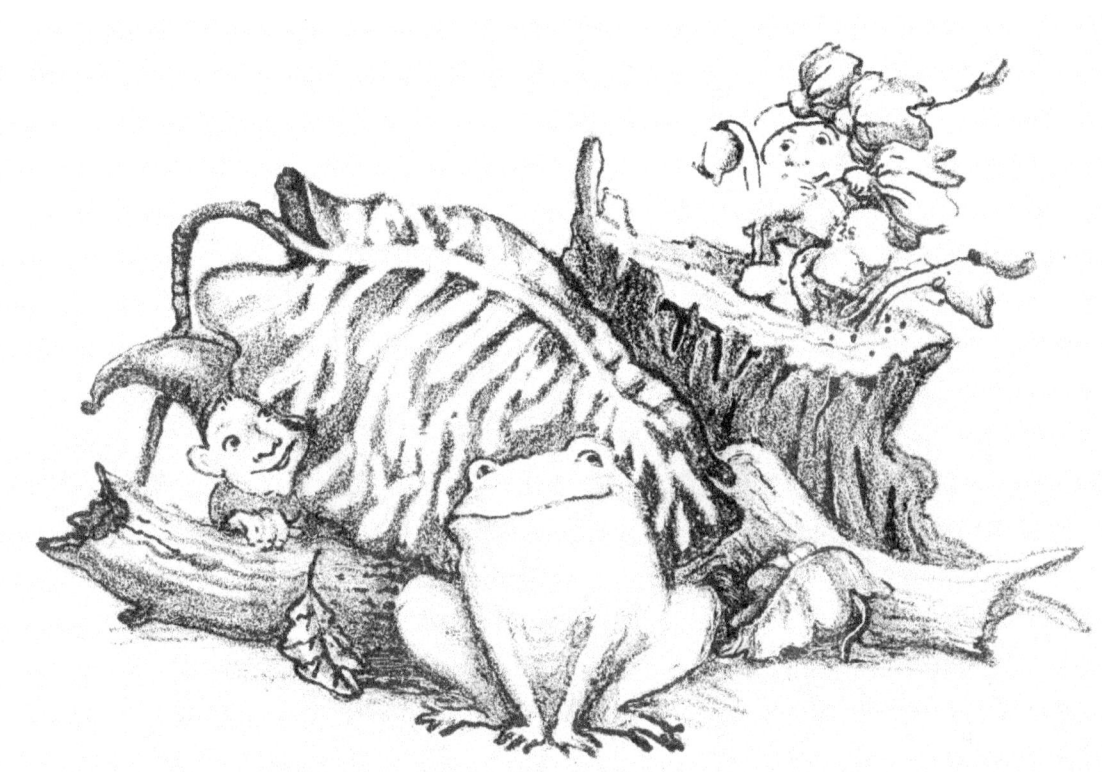

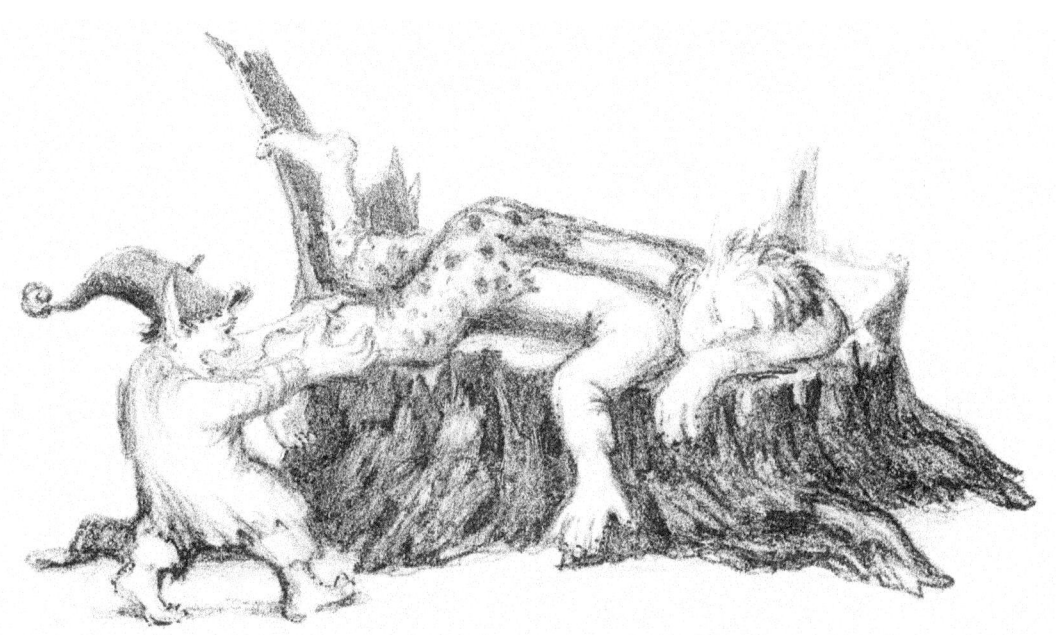

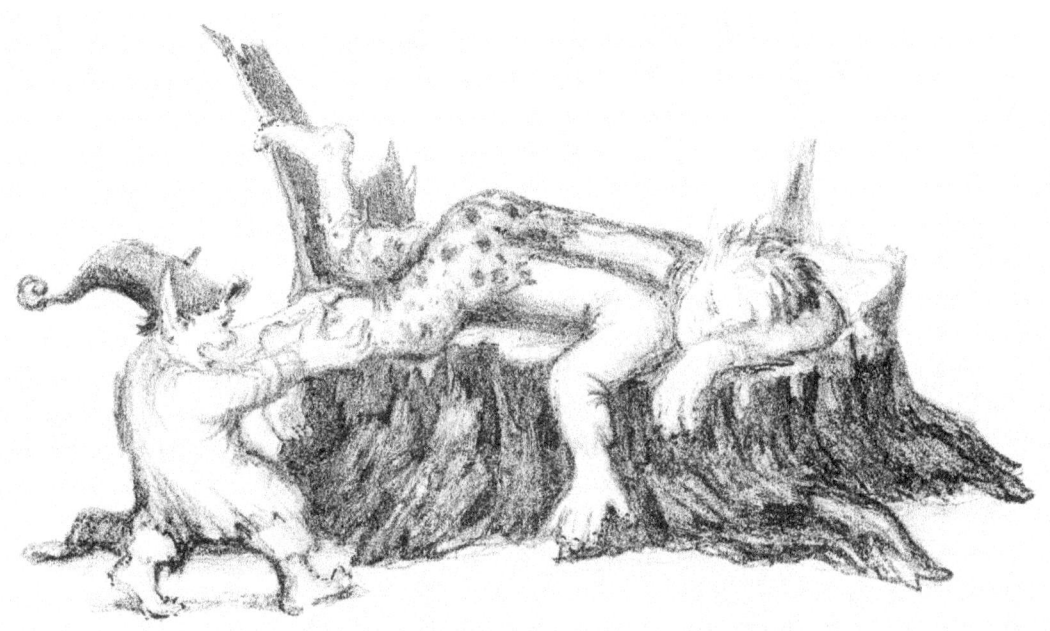

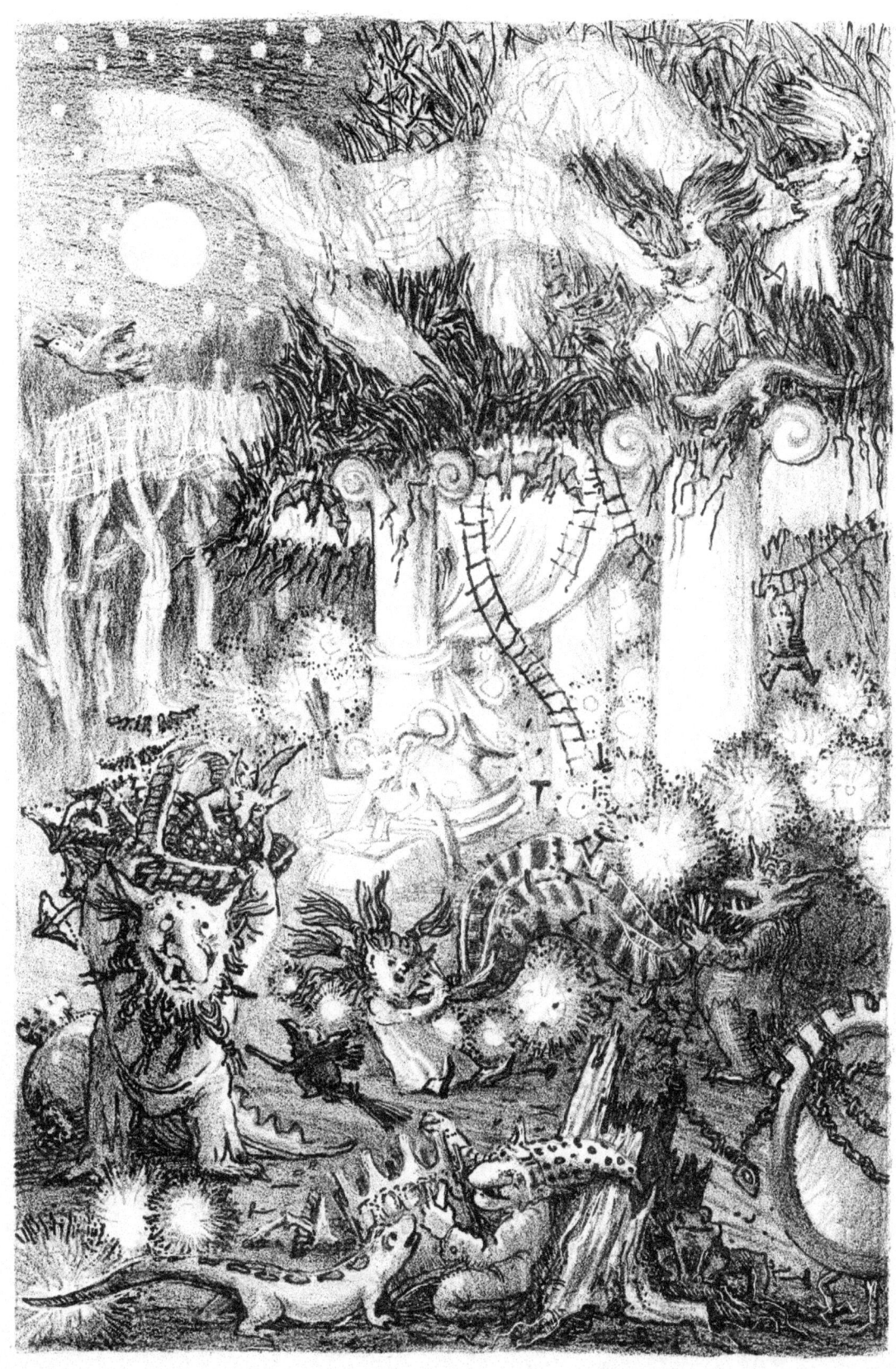

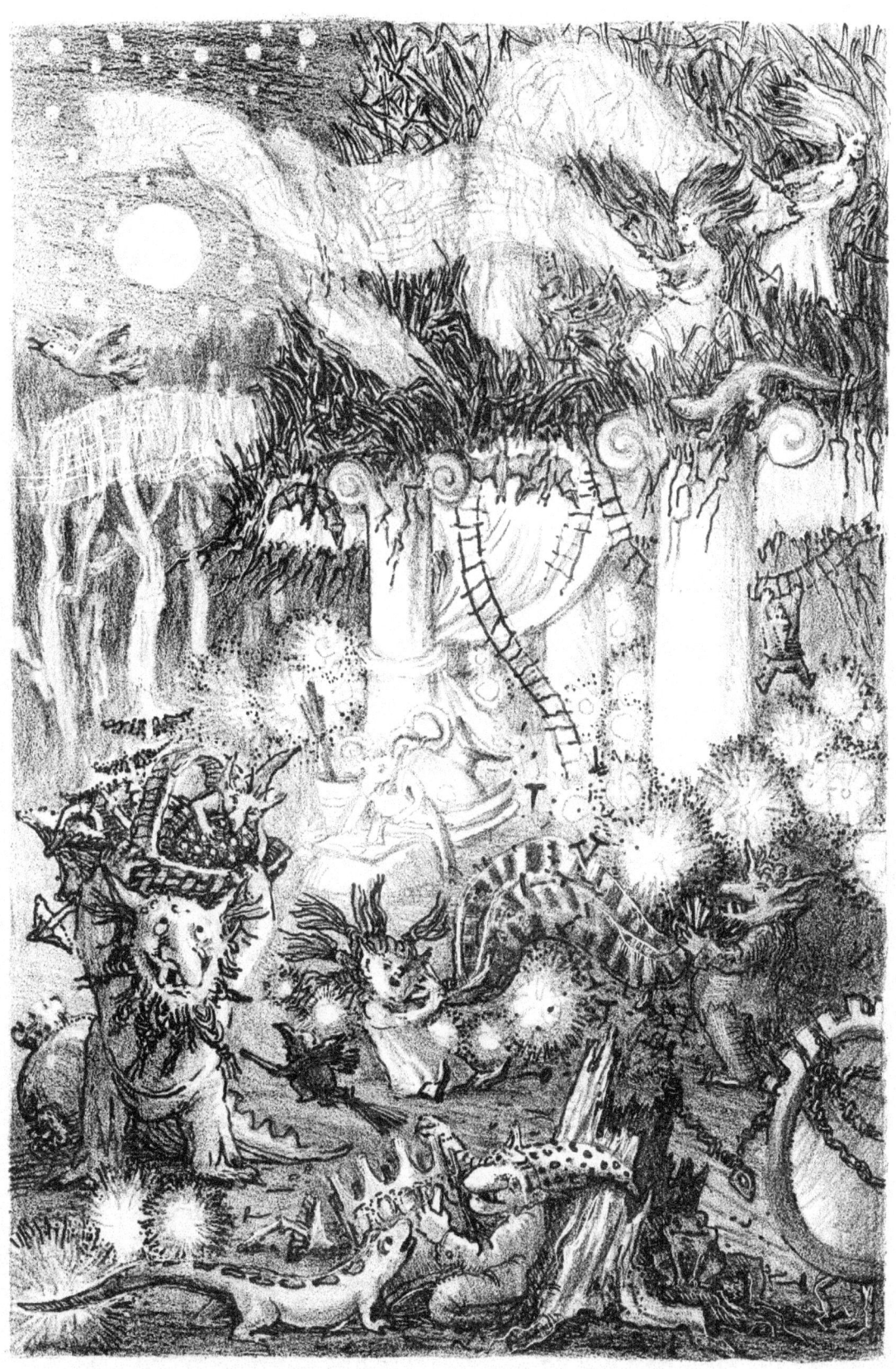

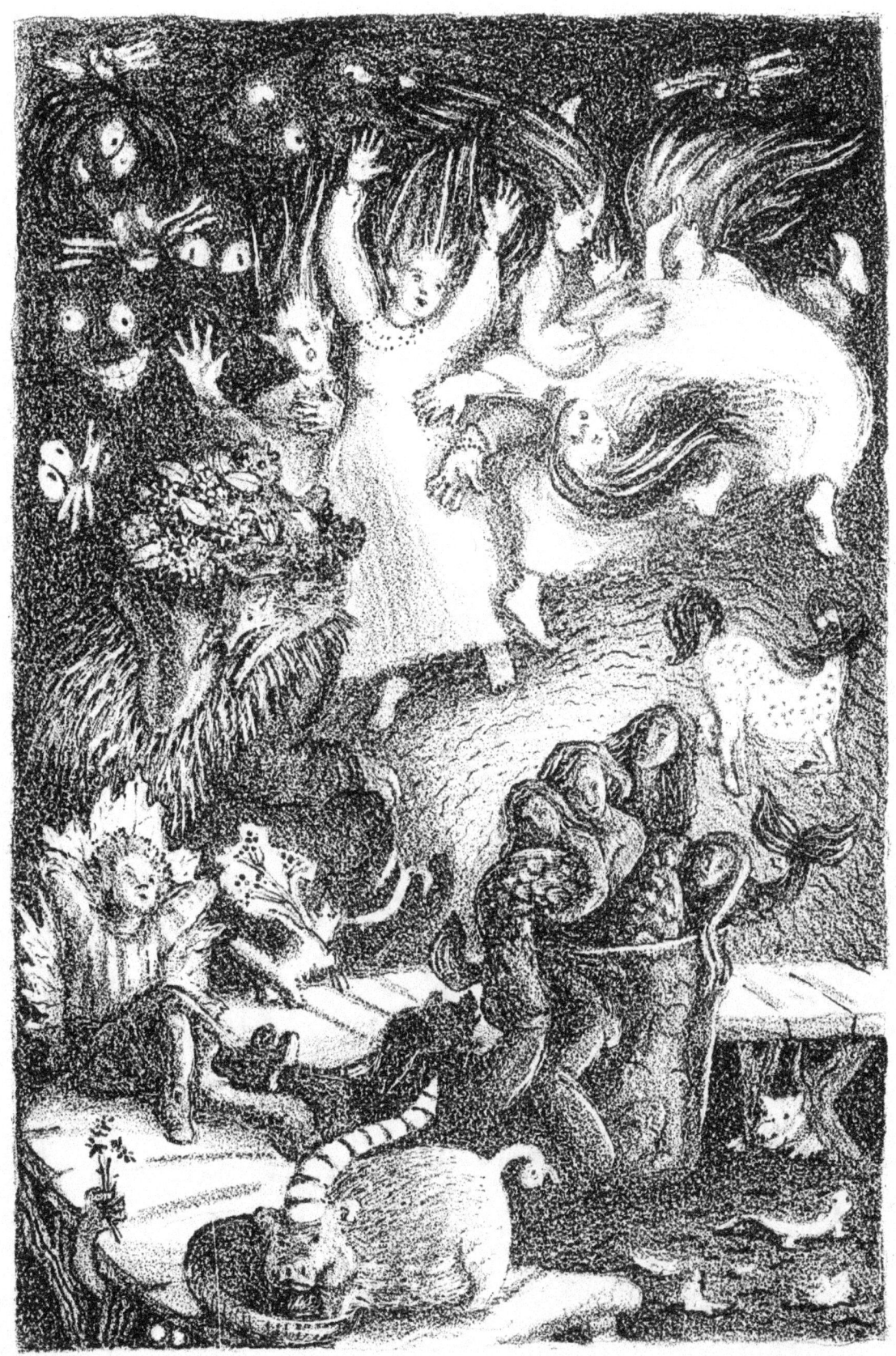

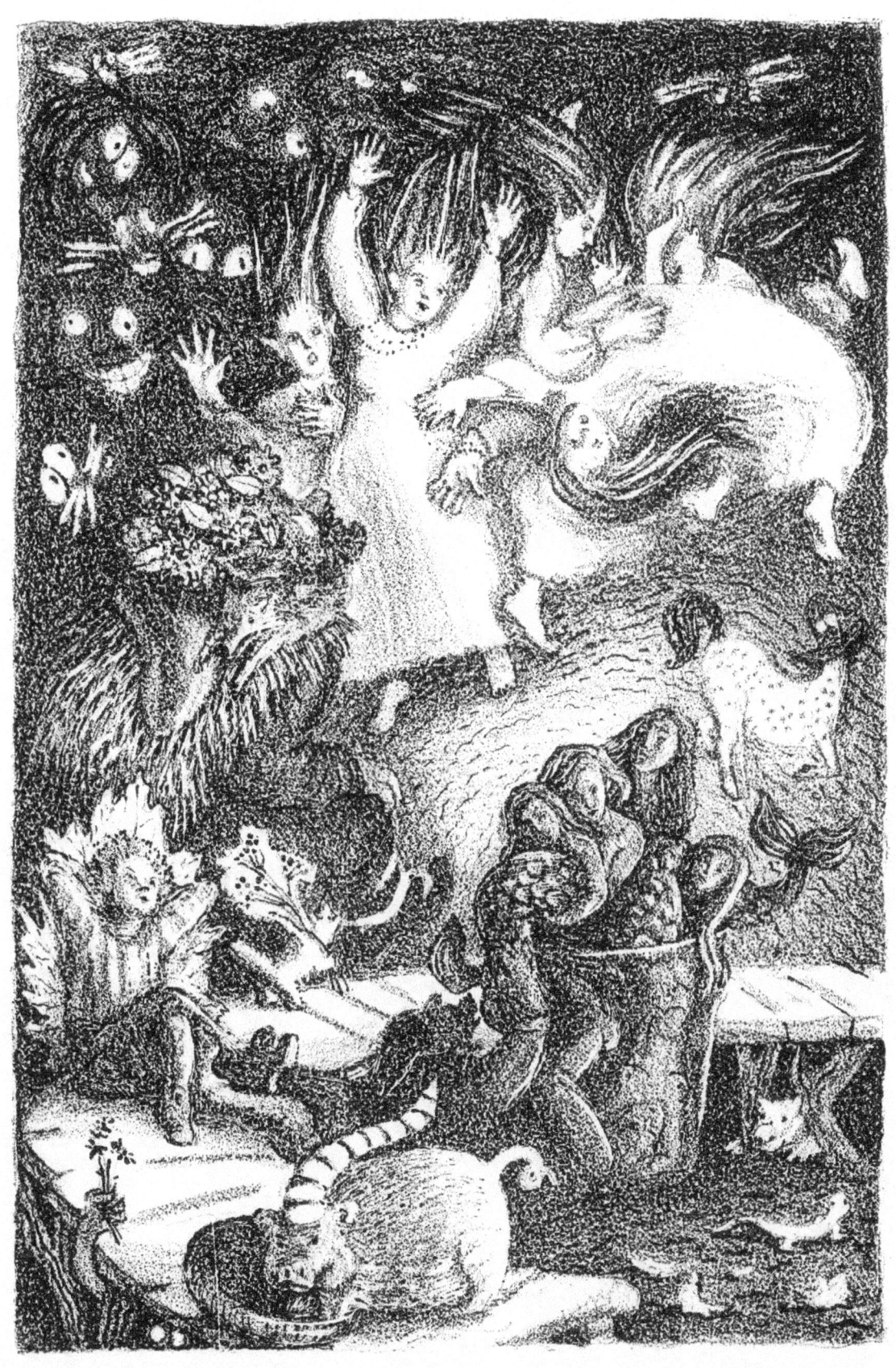

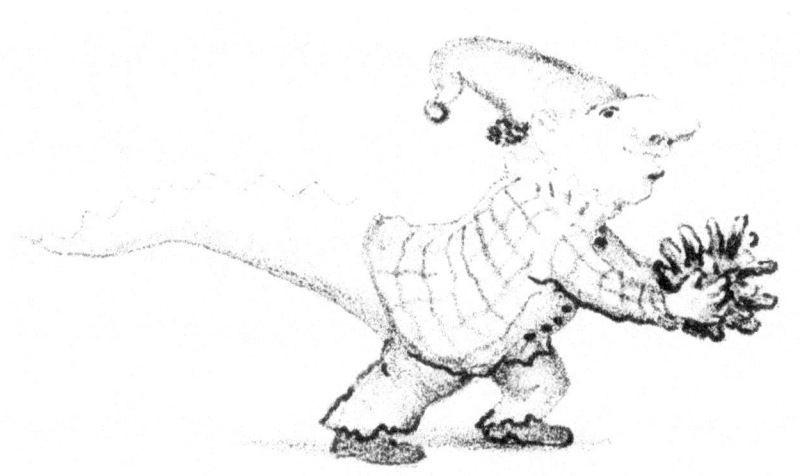

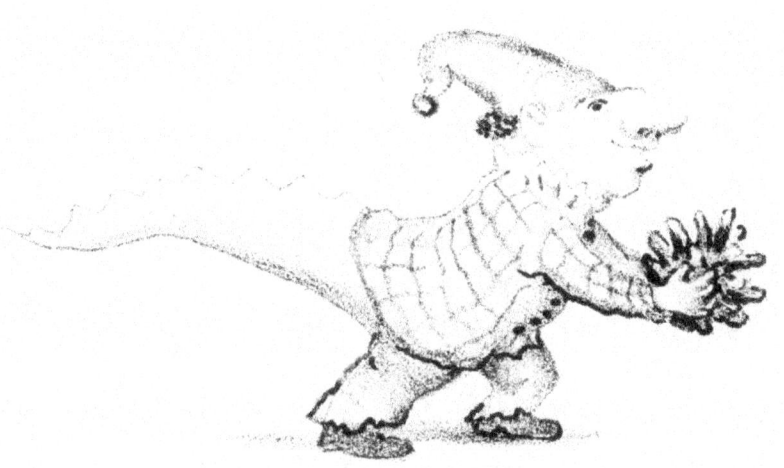

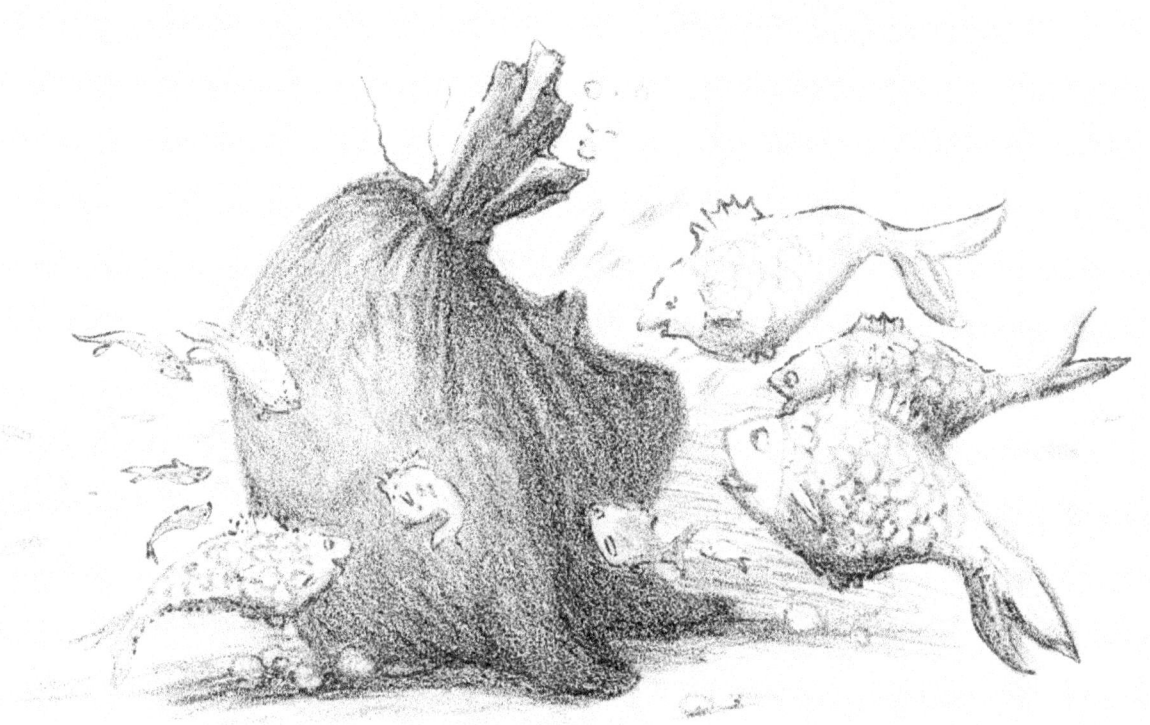

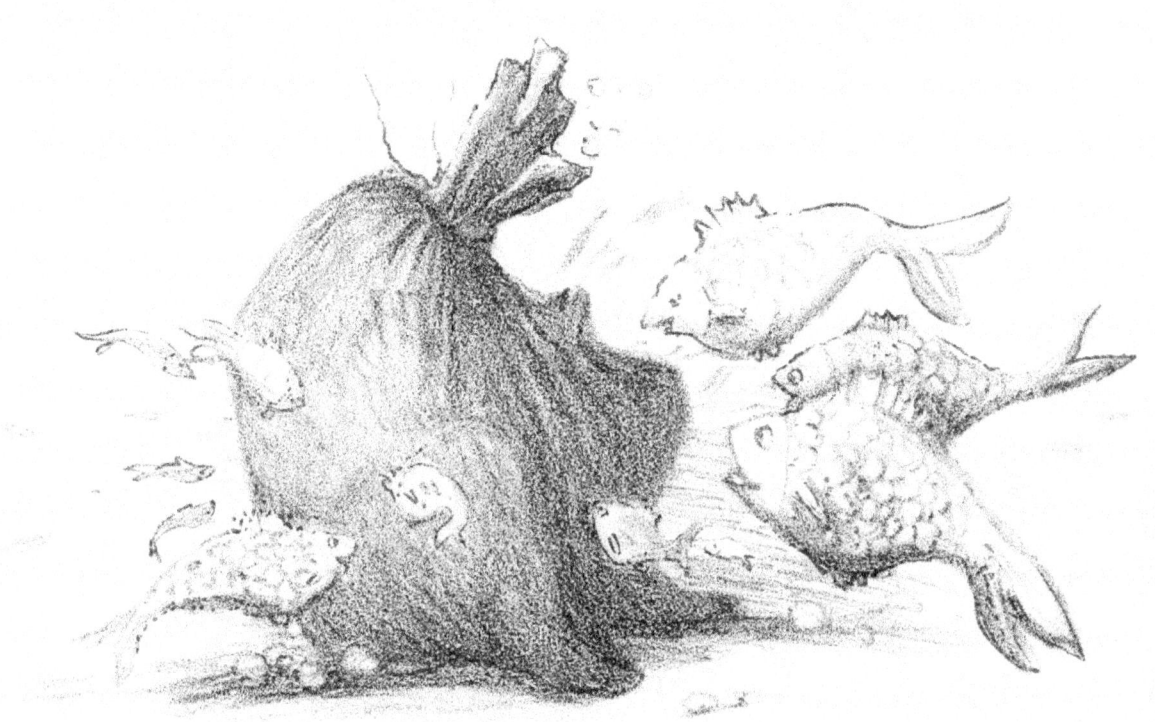